Managing Healthcare Ethically

Managing Healthcare Ethically

THIRD EDITION

VOLUME 3

Clinical
Challenges

ACHE Management Series

William A. Nelson | Paul B. Hofmann | Editors

Your board, staff, or clients may also benefit from this book's insight. For information on quantity discounts, contact the Health Administration Press Marketing Manager at (312) 424-9450.

This publication is intended to provide accurate and authoritative information in regard to the subject matter covered. It is sold, or otherwise provided, with the understanding that the publisher is not engaged in rendering professional services. If professional advice or other expert assistance is required, the services of a competent professional should be sought.

The statements and opinions contained in this book are strictly those of the authors and do not represent the official positions of the American College of Healthcare Executives or the Foundation of the American College of Healthcare Executives.

26 25 24 23 22   5 4 3 2 1

Library of Congress Cataloging-in-Publication Data
Names: Nelson, William A., editor. | Hofmann, Paul B., 1941– editor.
Title: Managing healthcare ethically / William A. Nelson, Paul B. Hofmann, editors.
Other titles: Management series (Ann Arbor, Mich.)
Description: Third edition. | Chicago, IL : Health Administration Press, [2022] | Series: HAP/ACHE management series | Includes bibliographical references. | Contents: v. 1. Leadership roles and responsibilities — v. 2. Organizational concerns — v. 3. Clinical challenges. | Summary: "This book discusses the numerous and complex issues that healthcare executives encounter every day as an intrinsic part of organizational life"— Provided by publisher.
Identifiers: LCCN 2021023677 (print) | LCCN 2021023678 (ebook) | ISBN 9781640552500 (v. 1 ; paperback ; alk. paper) | ISBN 9781640552555 (v. 2 ; paperback ; alk. paper) | ISBN 9781640552609 (v. 3 ; paperback ; alk. paper) | ISBN 9781640552470 (v. 1 ; epub) | ISBN 9781640552487 (v. 1 ; mobi) | ISBN 9781640552524 (v. 2 ; epub) | ISBN 9781640552531 (v. 2 ; mobi) | ISBN 9781640552579 (v. 3 ; epub) | ISBN 9781640552586 (v. 3 ; mobi)
Subjects: MESH: Health Services Administration—ethics | Leadership
Classification: LCC RA971 (print) | LCC RA971 (ebook) | NLM W 84.1 | DDC 362.1068—dc23
LC record available at https://lccn.loc.gov/2021023677
LC ebook record available at https://lccn.loc.gov/2021023678

The paper used in this publication meets the minimum requirements of American National Standard for Information Sciences—Permanence of Paper for Printed Library Materials, ANSI Z39.48-1984. ∞™

Acquisitions editor: Jennette McClain; Project manager: Andrew Baumann; Cover designer: Book Buddy Media; Layout: Integra

Found an error or a typo? We want to know! Please e-mail it to hapbooks@ache.org, mentioning the book's title and putting "Book Error" in the subject line.

For photocopying and copyright information, please contact Copyright Clearance Center at www.copyright.com or at (978) 750-8400.

Health Administration Press
A division of the Foundation of the American
    College of Healthcare Executives
300 S. Riverside Plaza, Suite 1900
Chicago, IL 60606-6698
(312) 424-2800

Contents

Foreword

THE AMERICAN COLLEGE OF Healthcare Executives' *Code of Ethics*—a defining document for ACHE and our members—states, "The fundamental objectives of the healthcare management profession are to maintain or enhance the overall quality of life, dignity and well-being of every individual needing healthcare service and to create an equitable, accessible, effective and efficient healthcare system." Healthcare executives have a responsibility to address ethical issues at broad organizational, community and societal levels through systematic processes. It is up to us as leaders to ensure an ethics-focused culture is in place, providing a foundation for policies, performance measures and management behavior, as well as clinician and patient interactions.

Since 1992, the "Healthcare Management Ethics" column in ACHE's *Healthcare Executive* magazine has been providing our members and the field with guidance on how to navigate myriad ethical issues. The editors of this new edition, William A. Nelson, PhD, HFACHE, and Paul B. Hofmann, DrPH, LFACHE, have regularly contributed to the column for more than 20 years and are recognized experts in healthcare management ethics. The columns they included in the third volume of *Managing Healthcare Ethically* examine challenges related to clinical care, such as informed consent, conflicts of interest, healthcare provider stress and burnout, addressing medical errors and end-of-life care.

Healthcare leaders are given a great privilege: to help care for people when they are at their most vulnerable. The columns that comprise this third volume serve as a necessary beacon in times and situations of uncertainty to help us deserve this honor.

I have personally known Bill and Paul for many years and am familiar with their great work in the field of healthcare management ethics. I am grateful for their adept curation in this new edition. Their wisdom, along with that of the other column contributors, has served as an indispensable source of guidance for ACHE members and for the field as a whole.

At ACHE, we strive to lead by example with an enduring commitment to ethics in advocacy and action. As such, we have interwoven an ethics-focused culture into the fabric of our organization. We encourage our members, as leaders in their organizations, to take an active role in the development and demonstration of ethical decision-making as it relates to all facets of healthcare management, but especially as it pertains to the clinical care you provide.

Deborah J. Bowen, FACHE, CAE
President and CEO
American College of Healthcare Executives

Acknowledgments

We WANT TO EXPRESS our appreciation to the many authors who have contributed to this book. Their efforts were essential to this edition, as they were to the two previous editions published by Health Administration Press in 2001 and 2010.

We also want to acknowledge the editors of the American College of Healthcare Executive (ACHE) publications that continue to publish articles on ethical topics. These articles are as vital to the leaders of today's healthcare organizations as they are to the educators preparing the leaders of tomorrow.

We would like to express our sincere gratitude to the Health Administration Press team, in particular Jennette McClain for her ongoing encouragement and support throughout the process of publishing this book and Andrew Baumann for his editing assistance.

Finally, we thank Deborah J. Bowen, FACHE, CAE, president and CEO of ACHE, for her unwavering commitment and leadership in supporting the essential role of ethics in the delivery of healthcare and in the education of healthcare executives.

Introduction

THIS IS THE THIRD of three volumes that constitute the third edition of *Managing Healthcare Ethically*, which builds on the two previous editions published by Health Administration Press in 2001 and 2010. Like the first two volumes, this one gathers selected columns originally written for American College of Healthcare Executives publications (primarily *Healthcare Executive* magazine), adding some provocative discussion questions and other material useful for teaching purposes. Here, we have collected columns that describe programs and processes that are helpful to executives in navigating through the often-daunting landscape that constitutes healthcare's new reality.

This volume focuses on common, recurring clinical ethics issues. Clinical ethics is a practical discipline that provides health professionals with a structured approach to identifying, analyzing, and resolving ethical issues that arise in clinical practice. These ethical challenges relate to conflicts that occur in the care and management of individual patients and groups of patients in today's healthcare institutions. Traditionally, clinical ethics issues relate to matters of informed consent, confidentiality and privacy, decision-making capacity or competence, decisions involving minors, and end-of-life care. This volume also includes several columns that explore the important role that ethics committees perform in developing and applying policies involving these issues.

Instructor Resources

This book's instructor resources include PowerPoint slides, case studies, and lists of selected ethics center websites and selected ethics journals.

For the most up-to-date information about this book and its instructor resources, go to ache.org/HAP and browse for the book's title, author name, or order code (24391).

This book's instructor resources are available to instructors who adopt this book for use in their course. For access information, please e-mail hapbooks@ache.org.

The Ethics of Telemedicine

William A. Nelson, PhD, HFACHE

VARIOUS HEALTHCARE TECHNOLOGIES ARE increasingly being recognized as essential tools to enhance the quality of patient care. The desire to broaden access to needed healthcare in the United States during the past two decades has resulted in the growing application of one specific form of health technology—telemedicine or telehealth. For example, the application of telemedicine has enhanced rural patients' access to specialists, including mental health professionals, cardiologists and dermatologists.

In addition to real-time, patient–provider telemedicine, several other uses of the technologies have developed for providers who are geographically separated, such as storage and transfer of clinical data and images; full-motion video from one site to another for the purpose of rendering a medical opinion; diagnosis functions including radiology, pathology, dermatology or ophthalmology; and home telemedicine. The Department of Veterans Affairs has made extensive use of all such technologies.

Telemedicine is also used for education, and in some locations—where there are limited ethics resources—telemedicine technology has even been used to provide healthcare professionals with ethics consultation.

Patients in general have expressed satisfaction with telemedicine because of the focused and uninterrupted attention they get from virtual healthcare providers. Providers have also been satisfied with telemedicine as an effective method to expand the reach of care. From a technological and evidence-based standpoint, it would appear that the virtual visit is a reliable and appropriate extension of traditional face-to-face contact.

ETHICAL CONCERNS

Despite widespread growth in the application of telemedicine there are limited publications on the ethical issues related to this dynamic technology. Just as there is ongoing evaluation and assessment of the application of telemedicine from both the patient and provider perspective, there also needs to be ongoing reflection on the ethical implications.

The telemedicine encounter should be guided by the same ethical principles that serve as the underpinning of all clinician–patient relationships. However, clinicians and healthcare executives need to recognize and address the *specific* ethical concerns that relate to the contextual nature of providing healthcare with a virtual methodology.

Following are some aspects of the telemedicine encounter that require ethical sensitivity from both administrators and clinicians.

INFORMED CONSENT

Autonomy requires clinicians to respect the patient's right to make an informed choice about participating in a telemedicine interaction. Involved caregivers must also ensure patients have a clear and complete understanding of the telemedicine method of care, including information about the security and use of personal data. Ideally a trusted local provider, such as a nurse practitioner facilitating the contact with the virtual provider, will describe the telemedicine system to the patient and clarify any questions regarding its application. Written material describing the telemedicine system is also useful and should be made readily available to patients.

In addition to giving general consent to participate in telemedicine, patients will need to give further valid consents regarding their acceptance of specific procedures or treatments by the virtual provider, such as a close-up photograph of a skin disorder or psychotherapy. If the recommended treatment is being provided by the local healthcare provider, then he/she will likely obtain or participate in the patient's consent process.

PRIVACY AND CONFIDENTIALITY

Of significant concern in telemedicine is patient privacy and confidentiality. The ethical concept of respect for the patient requires that clinicians ensure the privacy of every encounter and confidentiality of any personal information shared during the virtual exchange unless the patient requests or gives permission to have personal information shared.

Violations of privacy and confidentiality can be both visual and auditory. Breeches may be quite accidental and innocent, such as staff curiosity or when a passerby inadvertently views or hears a provider's or patient's telemedicine interactions. To foster privacy, the physical location of the patient–clinician interaction should occur in a setting that is not openly accessible to others, such as a closed room.

As telemedicine becomes more widely available and applied, clinicians and organization leadership should carefully plan strategies to ensure nonauthorized viewing of the patient–clinician encounter or personal information does not occur.

PROVIDER–PATIENT RELATIONSHIP

Telemedicine user and advocate David A. Fleming, MD, has raised the question whether its use might negatively impact the power of the provider–patient relationship. In an October 2009 *Telemedicine and e-Health* journal article, Fleming and his coauthors write: "The impact of the physician's presence and touch on the patient–physician relationship and the perception of patients when responding to face-to-face interactions have been demonstrated and cannot be discounted." Fleming and others have expressed concern that telemedicine as an innovative, growing technology may depersonalize and diminish the trust that defines the relationship between patients and healthcare providers.

This is an important concern, and it needs to be assessed through patient satisfaction surveys and regular reviews to ensure the integrity of the provider–patient relationship and its foundational ethical principles of trust and mutual respect are not diminished. Patients need to feel comfortable with the technology and the healthcare provider they are seeing on the screen. The patient's local provider, such as a physician or nurse, can foster a positive telemedicine relationship with the virtual provider by being with the patient, especially in the early stage of the telemedicine encounter, to help clarify any of the patient's concerns and introduce the distant provider.

For the distant provider, all the same aspects of a constructive, positive face-to-face patient–provider encounter should be captured in a telemedicine relationship. The healthcare professional must understand the patient's complaints, underlying feelings, goals and expectations and act responsibly. He or she must treat the patient with compassion and respect. The concern of a depersonalized relationship can be diminished when the provider's work carefully balances the coalition of knowledge, clinical skill and effective communication to attain the ultimate goal of fostering the patient's health.

To this end, Kenneth V. Iserson, MD, proposed in a July 2000 *Cambridge Quarterly for Healthcare Ethics* article that clinicians commit themselves to a telemedicine code of ethics that seeks to ensure that the integrity of patient–professional relationships is maintained. The useful code reinforces the key elements of an ethics-grounded provider–patient relationship for telemedicine-based care.

EQUITABLE ACCESS TO TELEMEDICINE

Rural Americans encounter a unique combination of factors that create disparities in healthcare not found in urban areas. As noted by the National Rural Health Association (www.ruralhealthweb.org), economic factors, cultural and social differences, educational shortcomings and the sheer isolation of living in remote rural areas all conspire to impede rural Americans in their struggle to lead normal, healthy lives.

For example, only about 10 percent of physicians practice in rural America despite the fact that nearly one-fourth of the population lives in these areas. The application of telemedicine technology has the potential to assist in decreasing current healthcare disparities in access to services and providers. Through the application of telemedicine in small, rural hospitals or clinics, patients can access an expanded range of specialists.

Unfortunately, the application of telemedicine as a driver for reducing healthcare disparities is only theoretical for many rural settings because they lack the required funds to purchase and maintain the technology. To provide needed care, executives and clinicians should explore various local, federal and state funding possibilities to foster equitable, quality healthcare. As a methodology to foster greater access to healthcare, telemedicine is still evolving. It has been shown to be a beneficial tool to expand accessibility and availability of healthcare to those who historically have lacked needed care. When using telemedicine, clinicians must never sway from their moral obligations to serve the patients' needs and act in their best interests. The effectiveness of telemedicine programs will ultimately depend on maintaining the ethical precepts that underpin the healthcare professional–patient relationship.

Originally published in the November/December 2010 issue of *Healthcare Executive* magazine.

Discussion Questions

Along with the widespread growth of telemedicine is the recognition of unique ethical challenges arising in its application. The author describes a few of those challenges. What additional challenges do you believe need attention?

Telemedicine programs tend to focus on individual patient care. What are some opportunities to apply the technology to promote population health?

Addressing the Second Victims of Medical Error

William A. Nelson, PhD, HFACHE

A SURGEON OPERATES ON the left knee when the problem is located on the right knee. A nurse administers the wrong medication to a patient. Based on a radiologist's incorrect report, an oncologist presents a cancer diagnosis to the wrong patient. A nursing aid fails to put a patient's bed rail in place and the patient falls and breaks a hip.

These examples reflect unintentional actions; mistakes or accidents that lead to medical errors. Each of these tragic errors significantly impacts the quality of patient care and the organization's reputation. To address medical errors, the number of patient safety programs within healthcare organizations has grown significantly, accelerated by the publication of the Institute of Medicine's 1999 report, *To Err Is Human: Building a Safer Health System.*

The report, which found that medical errors are responsible for between 44,000 and 98,000 preventable deaths every year in healthcare delivery, continues to serve as a dramatic wake-up call for healthcare organizations to aggressively seek approaches to reducing medical errors. Unfortunately, even since the report's publication and the subsequent growth of patient safety programs, medical errors continue to be a significant problem in today's healthcare organizations.

Following an adverse event, as medical errors are commonly described, many organizations immediately, and correctly, focus their attention on the victim—the patient. In the cases described above, the patient clearly suffers from the error and is the primary victim. Many ethicists have convincingly reasoned that transparency regarding the disclosure of a medical error is the appropriate course of action. Most healthcare facilities currently have policies or guidelines outlining a process for disclosing medical errors to patients and, in some cases, patients' family members. Some debate still remains regarding the extent of this disclosure, such as whether an error that does not lead to an adverse outcome should be disclosed to the patient.

Some organizations have internal reporting systems when an error is not actually committed but almost; these "near misses" are also reviewed. Despite some of the remaining debates over reporting and disclosure guidelines, the general concept of reporting medical errors within organizations and disclosing errors to patients and their families is widely accepted. Healthcare organizations are also affected by a professional's error; it can negatively affect their institutional culture, reputation and, in some situations, result in costly litigation. Medical errors can be economically costly and compromise the patient's trust in the healthcare system and the involved professionals. To address these concerns, healthcare organizations should aggressively pursue the causes of medical errors.

The IOM report suggests most errors are not caused by "individual recklessness. . . . More commonly, errors are caused by faulty systems, processes and conditions that lead people to make mistakes or fail to prevent them." Discovering why an error occurred is the starting place for the implementation of a system-oriented quality improvement approach to diminishing the recurrence of errors and to providing support for the victims of medical error, including the second victims.

THE SECOND VICTIMS

Errors commonly result from a breakdown in the healthcare delivery system and, thus, the actions of several healthcare professionals working together as a team. These individual professionals can be considered the "second victims" of medical errors, as they often suffer emotionally and physically as a result of the adverse outcome. The impact of the medical error on these healthcare providers can be substantial, affecting their personal lives, interactions with colleagues and professional confidence.

The second victim typically experiences deep stress that includes physical symptoms such as sleep disturbance, crying and headaches. Emotional stress may be manifested in feelings of sadness, fear, anger, shame and damage to professional self-esteem. As the organization reviews the error, the second victim can be plagued by self-doubt and a loss of confidence in the workplace. Second victims may be plagued by questions of professional insecurity, fearful that their reputations will continue to suffer as a result of their competence being questioned.

Additionally, stress levels among the colleagues of second victims may rise. Healthcare professionals may be concerned about making similar errors in their work, or they may worry that they contributed to or could have prevented their colleague's error. Co-workers may have concerns about communicating with the individual who made the error, especially if they are concerned about privacy and legal considerations. Or, they simply may not know how to be supportive.

In a 2009 article in the journal *BMJ Quality and Safety*, Susan D. Scott and colleagues describe how after a medical error, clinical confidence was further eroded by non-supportive and negative comments that resulted in difficulty restoring the second victim's professional and personal integrity. Clinicians and administrative leadership must understand that medical errors can and will occur in today's complex healthcare organizations and, subsequently, how to manage and support colleagues who are involved in errors.

Scott and colleagues have shown that following a medical error, second victims experience a series of stages in their recovery: "1) chaos and accident response, 2) intrusive reflections, 3) restoring personal integrity, 4) enduring the inquisition, 5) obtaining emotional first aid, and, 6) moving on." The last two stages are particularly noteworthy for healthcare executives. Scott's research suggests that the "moving on" stage can play out in three distinct paths:

- **Dropping out:** changing one's professional role, profession or work site
- **Surviving:** doing OK professionally and performing as expected while still plagued by the event
- **Thriving:** being involved with practice change or redesign, making something good come out of the unfortunate event

The pain, suffering and potential outcome paths from the "moving on" process reported by second victims should prompt leaders and supervisory managers of any organization to consider and plan for how clinicians who make errors will be supported when they occur. Healthcare professionals are too valuable of an asset to lose as a result of an unintentional error.

CARING FOR SECOND VICTIMS

Just as organizations need to create an ethics-based culture of quality and safety, an organization has a moral responsibility to foster the healing and recovery of second victims. Healthcare leaders should critically examine and develop strategies that support clinicians when errors occur, providing what Scott and colleagues call "first aid." Comprehensive support can make the difference between a professional "dropping out" and "thriving."

Healthcare organizations must develop a formal effort that promotes open discussions of the issues surrounding second victims. Support for second victims must begin immediately after the event and extend for as long as is necessary. For example, managers and front-line supervisors can be trained to initiate support during the early stages following an error. Organizational resources, such as social workers, risk managers, mental health providers, employee health professionals and chaplains, also need to be trained to respond to second victims in an appropriate and timely manner.

Organized support for second victims is rare in most healthcare facilities, but there are a few outstanding examples. In 2010 The Johns Hopkins Hospital launched a Second Victims Committee aimed at assisting caregivers who are traumatized as a result of unexpected patient outcomes and errors.

In 2009, the patient safety officer at University of Missouri Health Care created the "forYOU Team," which provides one-on-one peer support for the clinician or group of professionals affected by a medical error. Members of the peer support team go through specialized training, including role-playing, to learn how to better assist their colleagues. Members meet monthly for case reviews and work closely with legal counsel.

These all too few examples reflect organizations fulfilling their morally grounded focus on not only their patients but also their staff members. When second victims are ignored or abandoned by their organizations, they suffer alone, and their suffering can be a wound that infects the organization's overall culture. A healthcare organization that focuses on the care of both the first and second victims of medical errors reflects an ethically grounded organization with a caring culture.

Originally published in the March/April 2013 issue of *Healthcare Executive* magazine.

Discussion Questions

Despite strong institutional safety programs to reduce medical errors, they continue to occur. What is the impact on the person who has committed a medical error?

Assuming organizations have a moral obligation to support individuals who have committed a medical error, what is the best approach for assisting these individuals, and why?

Admitting Errors Is the Right Thing to Do

William A. Nelson, PhD, HFACHE

THE MAJOR PUSH TO recognize and reduce medical errors is more than 15 years old, beginning by most estimates with the publication of the Institute of Medicine's (now named The National Academies of Sciences, Engineering and Medicine) 1999 report *To Err Is Human.* Soon after came an explosion in the development of patient safety offices seeking system-oriented approaches to reduce errors.

Along with the recognition of the extent to which medical errors exist came a growing campaign around communicating with patients and their families regarding medical errors. The journey to full and open disclosure of medical errors, reflecting an approach of transparency, continues today.

ESTABLISHING A MEDICAL ERROR POLICY

Even before the landmark report, a few healthcare organizations explored disclosure initiatives; however, there were few public discussions about such efforts, as most were not part of a formal program. Additionally, little was known about the impact of such initiatives.

That began to change in 1999, when Steve Kraman, MD, a medical director for the Veterans Affairs Medical Center in Lexington, Kentucky, and Ginny Hamm, JD, an attorney and a member of the hospital's ethics committee, published a paper in *Annals of Internal*

Medicine describing the disclosure program at the medical center. To the surprise of many skeptics, there was no significant increase in the number of claims or payouts after the disclosure program was initiated. The paper stirred much discussion among healthcare leaders. However, despite the authors' findings and a well-reasoned ethical foundation for the program, there continued to be pushback to the program from some legal counsel and administrative and clinical leaders.

The journey to full disclosure accelerated in 2001 after The Joint Commission issued a nationwide disclosure standard requiring that patients be informed about outcomes of care, including unanticipated outcomes. Additionally, some states have passed disclosure-related legislation. These standards have fostered the widespread development of disclosure policies throughout the country.

Underpinning the regulatory standards and need for organization disclosure policies is the goal to align physicians' and other healthcare professionals' actions with their ethical obligations. This includes their fiduciary responsibilities to act in the patient's best interest ahead of their own and the organization's and to support the right of patients to make informed decisions about their care based on a full understanding of their situation. Failure to disclose information is a form of deception that can lead to an undermining of trust in the organization and those who provide care.

The establishment of disclosure policies has continued to increase, ranging from simple restatements of The Joint Commission standards to policies describing detailed disclosure procedures. The development of a disclosure policy requires thoughtful collaboration among administrative and clinical leaders and should include the involvement of the organization's risk management and ethics committees. As Allen B. Kachalia, MD, JD, and David W. Bates, MD, indicated in their 2014 article in *The Surgeon,* "Today, disclosure is often regarded as a necessary part of transparency required to build greater patient trust and foster a stronger culture of safety. . . . By revealing our errors to our patients, we'll be better equipped to learn from our mistakes."

Despite the presence of policies that include a disclosure requirement, many organizations do not stipulate the scope and approach for disclosing medical errors. For healthcare executives and clinicians, having a policy that simply restates The Joint Commission standard is not enough. To foster real change in practice, the policy must outline detailed reporting and disclosure procedures. Organizations that clearly lay out disclosure protocols help to diminish the emotional and professional challenges that healthcare professionals encounter in such situations. Important considerations in the writing of disclosure practices, as noted by Thomas Gallagher, MD, and colleagues in a 2007 article in *The New England Journal of Medicine*, include the following:

- Disclosure of outcomes information to patients should be recognized as a core component of high-quality, respectful healthcare.
- Safe healthcare recognizes that disclosures are uniquely challenging conversations that call for appropriate staff preparation and support.
- The defined disclosure content should include a clear expression of regret and apology.

Once the policy is approved, a program should be planned, implemented and assessed to create an organization-wide culture of disclosure. Fundamental to any successful disclosure discussion program is an investment in training for all those involved, including clinicians, administrators and risk management professionals. Such training, however, should not be a one-time event; it must be ongoing. For example, there should be a debriefing following disclosure discussions to determine what went well during the disclosure process, what could be improved and what lessons were learned.

In some organizations that have established a disclosure policy, there appears to be a gap between policy and practice. For example, a colleague of mine described such an experience related to his wife's surgical procedure. His wife was undergoing abdominal surgery that was expected to last about an hour and a half. While waiting to hear the outcome of his wife's surgery, my colleague realized it had been several hours since the operation began. The surgeon finally appeared and escorted him to a private room, where the surgeon told my colleague that he could soon visit his wife in the recovery room. The surgeon indicated all was fine, but before the surgeon walked out of the room my friend noted that the procedure seemed to take much longer than expected. The surgeon replied, "We had a little issue, but all is OK." My friend quickly responded, "What do you mean, 'a little issue?'" The surgeon answered, "We had a little problem." My friend said, "Excuse me, doctor. What do you mean, 'a little problem?'" The surgeon then explained that the patient's bowel was accidentally nicked during the surgery, so that issue had to be addressed. The surgeon went on to explain what was done to address the complication. The accidental nick did delay discharge by one day; however, no further complications arose for my friend's wife. Still, a forthright discussion regarding what occurred during the surgery would have been more in line with the hospital's disclosure policy.

MOVING FROM POLICY TO PRACTICE

Despite the development of policies throughout the United States and in other countries, there continues to be a general hesitancy and, likely, lack of full compliance with an organization's policy due to litigation fears, the perceived negative impact on the organization and clinicians' reputation, and embarrassment.

The case of my colleague's wife highlights the challenges and reluctance of some clinicians to openly disclose a medical error, despite the presence of a disclosure policy. It is simply hard for clinicians—or anyone for that matter—to admit that an error or unanticipated problem occurred. A well-developed and defined disclosure procedure would empower clinicians to apply effective communication strategies with patients and their families. The procedure would guide them to focus on not only the facts of an error and what is being done to avoid it in the future, but also on the emotional aspects of the situation. Failure to acknowledge the feelings of patients and their families during the communication exchange can risk the patient, or in this case, the spouse, feeling as if the physician is uncaring and, worse yet, deceptive.

The problem of ensuring appropriate and timely disclosure is both an organizational and individual issue. Organizations must create the climate—a just culture—where healthcare professionals accept a full-disclosure approach and abide by it. Any organizational, professional or cultural barriers to effective disclosure should be recognized and addressed to ensure disclosure practices are fully implemented. Individuals must be nurtured and appropriately prepared and supported in adhering to the disclosure policy.

Administrative and clinical leaders also must recognize that telling a patient or family member about an error is highly emotional, and the message being communicated is very important. In the example shared earlier, the clinician's reluctance was apparent, and disclosure only occurred after the spouse continued to push for more information. The process most likely created even further concern for the spouse regarding the care delivered. As my friend indicated later, "I know errors happen, but what upset me was the effort I had to take to get the physician to disclose what happened."

Healthcare executives must create an environment in which the organization recognizes that disclosing error policies does not exist solely to fulfill a standard set by The Joint Commission. Instead, a medical error policy is an ethical value that should be embedded into the life of the organization. The full and consistent implementation of such policies can create an organizational shift away from a culture of nondisclosure and fear of recrimination to one of improving quality and safety through a systemwide focus on addressing the cause of medical errors.

Originally published in the July/August 2016 issue of *Healthcare Executive* magazine.

Discussion Questions

The establishment of a medical error organizational policy, including full disclosure to patients and their families, has been propagated ever since the 1999 publication of *To Err Is Human*. What is the ethical rationale for creating such policies?

Despite medical error policies, there appears to be a gap between having a policy and complying with it. What can be done to diminish this gap?

Boundary Issues in Rural America

William A. Nelson, PhD, HFACHE

OVERLAPPING PROFESSIONAL–PERSONAL RELATIONSHIPS ARE a common occurrence in rural America and can raise potential boundary ethics conflicts for providers and executives alike. These conflicts occur when healthcare professionals inappropriately cross the boundary limits of their relationships with patients as established by professional ethics standards, the law or organizational regulations. Boundary crossings are often associated with improper sexual relationships or contact between healthcare professionals and patients or employees. However, that is only one form of the boundary issues that may raise ethical concerns or violate ethical standards.

Focus groups with staff from rural facilities have described overlapping relationships as one of the most frequently encountered characteristics shaping rural life. Living or working in rural settings creates informal and formal face-to-face social interactions. It is an environment in which the patient is frequently a familiar person compared to the more anonymous patient living in an urban setting. In an illustrative example, a clinician described how she welcomed the opportunity to move from a large, urban medical center to a small, rural facility to serve as a primary care physician. She had encountered a broad array of ethical challenges in her previous position as a clinician and member of her organization's ethics program but felt unprepared for the frequency of boundary issues resulting from overlapping personal–professional contact with patients she experienced in the rural setting.

Rural providers have noted, "I go to church, there are my patients; when I drive in my neighborhood, I wave to patients." Or, "Many stop me when shopping and ask about their health issues. Sure, I can say, 'I will talk with you in the clinic,' but that does not reflect the values of the community nor does it feel comfortable to me." An administrator of an outpatient clinic described the questions that arose from other patients and staff members after they witnessed him giving a neighbor/patient a ride home at the end of the work day because he lacked other transportation.

These real-life descriptions reinforce the point that ethics questions are strongly influenced by the setting's context—in this case, rural America.

WHEN OVERLAPPING RELATIONSHIPS CREATE ETHICS CONFLICTS

Overlapping professional and personal relations are both challenging and complicated. Knowing a patient personally can enrich the clinical relationship between providers and patients because of familiarity with the patient's values; however, it also can create uncertainty and potential ethics issues related to the health professional's role, conflicts of interest, and questions regarding confidentiality and fiduciary commitment. In addition, an overlapping relationship can potentially compromise the clinician's or administrator's professional judgment and be perceived as showing favoritism. Furthermore, crossing professional boundaries not only harms the patient but can erode the trust and confidence others in the community have in the profession.

Looking to professional standards can be helpful; however, it is a challenge to apply such concepts in rural settings. As Laura Weiss Roberts, MD, and colleagues accurately noted in an article in the July/August 1999 issue of the *Hastings Center Report*, professional standards do not always account for the rural context, where patient contact in the community is unavoidable and expected. The determination whether an ethical professional boundary has been crossed must be reviewed within the unique rural context, where nonprofessional contact and social interaction are the norm and not inherently an ethical violation.

To help assess whether personal contact with a patient has raised an ethical conflict, a clinician or administrator should explore these questions:

- Might the personal relationship/contact alter your professional actions regarding the patient?
- Would the personal relationship/contact cause professional colleagues, other patients or community members to question your professional judgment and integrity?
- Would you want others to be aware of this overlapping personal and professional relationship/contact?
- Does the overlapping relationship/contact violate specific organizational or ethical guidelines?
- Is the extent of your overlapping relationship/contact a customary cultural expectation within the community?

In an article in the book *Educating for Professionalism: Creating a Culture of Humanism in Medical Education* (University of Iowa Press, 2000), Richard Martinez, MD, describes four types of behaviors that offer a wide variation of potential ethical risks, ranging from those behaviors that are criminally liable to those that pose a minimal risk, such as informal community conversations. Martinez's graded model of risk is a useful resource for analyzing the crossing of ethics boundaries.

ADDRESSING BOUNDARY CONFLICTS

Because boundary conflicts will inevitability occur, healthcare providers and executives in rural settings should employ a number of approaches to anticipate and address potential ethics conflicts:

Separate roles. To the extent possible healthcare professionals should try to separate their personal and professional roles when an interaction or encounter does occur. A physician may be at a dinner party with a patient/acquaintance or go fishing with a patient/friend. During the social contact, the physician can avoid discussing personal health issues and encourage the patient/friend or acquaintance to do likewise. Additionally, patients should be called "Mr." or "Mrs." in the professional context, even though first names are used during nonprofessional contact. This will help reinforce role distinctions.

Proactively discuss boundary conflicts with patients. Healthcare professionals should discuss this issue with their patients, who are or potentially will become personal acquaintances. Conversations can help diminish the potential awkwardness of having overlapping relationships and clarify the clinician's professional responsibilities. Such open communication can be beneficial for both the health provider and the patient.

Seek consultation with others. Professionals should discuss the issue of overlapping relationships with colleagues or their organization's ethics committee members. Explore with colleagues how they address community contact with patients. Be aware of any related organizational policies.

Transfer the patient. Consider transferring a patient, who is or has become a close friend, to another healthcare professional whenever possible.

Develop local boundary guidelines. As with other recurring ethics conflicts, healthcare executives, in collaboration with clinicians, should take a proactive, organizational approach to anticipating and decreasing potential overlapping relationship boundary issues. Such a proactive approach could lead to the development of an ethics practice guideline. A guideline is not meant to be a rigid, formal policy document—it can serve as a general guide to assist staff when encountering patients in nonprofessional situations.

A useful resource in drafting this guideline is the United States Department of Veterans Affairs' National Center for Ethics in Health Care 2003 report *Ethical Boundaries in the Patient–Clinician Relationship,* available at www.ethics.va.gov/pubs/necreports.asp. To propagate the guidelines within the organization, an education session should be conducted. This training should clarify the ethical reasoning for the guideline, offer relevant examples, and include role-playing so clinicians and executives can practice various approaches to handling patient encounters that occur outside the healthcare setting.

Write and propagate boundary guidelines. Rural facilities should include their guidelines regarding boundary issues in patient information booklets. What is communicated in these booklets should be based on professional standards and organizational policies such as privacy and confidentiality regulations.

Consider holding community forums. Many rural facilities have regular community forums on a wide range of topics, from smoking cessation to advance care planning. A community education forum could be an opportunity to openly discuss overlapping relationships and professionalism. The forum could be offered in collaboration with other community professionals, such as clergy, who frequently encounter a similar issue.

Encountering patients in nonprofessional situations is inevitable, and it is naive for nonrural professionals to think that such contact can or should be avoided. Clinicians and healthcare executives are not only members of a profession, but members of the community. Avoiding ethical conflicts caused by overlapping social relations requires a thoughtful balance between maintaining the integrity of the professional–patient relationship and still living and being socially engaged with some patients as friends and neighbors. Proactively addressing these conflicts can help reduce professional stress and uncertainty.

Originally published in the March/April 2010 issue of *Healthcare Executive* magazine.

Discussion Questions

Overlapping relations between healthcare professionals and the community served is a common occurrence in rural settings. Describe how such relationships can create ethics conflicts.

Offer several suggestions for mitigating potential conflicts of interest for clinicians.

Culture Clashes and Moral Judgments

Paul B. Hofmann, DrPH, LFACHE

THE ELDERLY CHINESE PATIENT had extensive metastatic cancer and moderate dementia, but he was alert, was communicative and seemed to have decision-making capacity. His wife had been designated his surrogate decision maker and had a durable power of attorney for healthcare. She told her husband's caregivers that she did not want him to know his diagnosis or prognosis.

In keeping with her family's cultural tradition, the patient's wife said this decision had been made by their eldest son. The other family members concurred because they felt the patient would become depressed if he was informed of his condition.

The hospital's staff members, however, thought the patient should be permitted to make a choice. Did he want to be aware of his disease and life expectancy, or would he prefer to have this information conveyed to his family and controlled by them? An ethics consult was requested by the patient's physician.

INCREASING CULTURAL DIVERSITY, INEVITABLE MORAL JUDGMENTS

Almost 20 percent of the American population spoke a language other than English at home in 2000. In July 2010, the American College of Physicians issued a policy paper titled *Racial and Ethnic*

Disparities in Health Care. With greater diversity, cultural competency will become more important as clinicians are confronted with different belief systems that "influence their ability or patient receptivity to provider recommendations," the authors said. While only half of all patients generally adhere to medical or prescription instructions offered by clinicians, rates of adherence are significantly lower for racial and ethnic minorities, according to the paper.

Compounding the growing challenge of effectively caring for our multicultural society is the largely ignored influence of patients who trigger moral judgments by physicians, nurses and other clinicians. Terry Hill, MD, a geriatrician in the Department of Medicine at the University of California, San Francisco, notes there is scant literature on the actual prevalence and dynamics of moral judgment in healthcare. In a July 9, 2010, article in the *Philosophy, Ethics, and Humanities in Medicine* journal he writes, "The paucity of attention to moral judgment, despite its significance for patient-centered care, communication, empathy, professionalism, healthcare education, stereotyping, and outcome disparities, represents a blind spot that merits explanation and repair."

Dr. Hill's insightful analysis is an eloquent call to action for healthcare leaders to recognize and address this vacuum. A proper response will assist both institutional and individual providers in becoming more culturally competent and more ethically sensitive caregivers. The three-volume publication *Doorway Thoughts: Cross-Cultural Health Care for Older Adults*, published by the American Geriatric Society, is only one example of a superb resource to facilitate the educational process.

OUTCOME OF ETHICS CONSULT

Following a discussion about the elderly Chinese patient's case, the Ethics Committee recommended "transparent confirmation" be obtained from the patient to verify his preference that information regarding his diagnosis and prognosis should be conveyed only to his family. The attending physician agreed with the committee's recommendation. In an informal discussion with the patient and his family present, she indicated her understanding that the patient preferred (a) not to be informed of his clinical condition, (b) to have such information provided to his family and (c) to continue to have decisions regarding his treatment made by his wife. The patient confirmed this was his preference.

Regardless of the circumstances, it is usually difficult to withhold information from a competent patient. This case illustrates the "medical culture clash" that can occur between family members and staff members. Determining the right thing to do is not easy, though, because there is no one right answer to these dilemmas. The resolution requires a thoughtful process that permits competing values to be reconciled.

Respecting patient and family choices is a fundamental component of the ethical principle of autonomy. In a previous article ("When Patients Make 'Unwise' Decisions," published in the June 13, 2006, issue of *Hospitals & Health Networks* online), I argued that we should recognize who is labeling a patient's decision as "unwise." Certainly, it is not the patient. I said we should realize that describing a patient's decision as unwise is itself laden with judgment.

For example, a severely ill patient may refuse a commonly accepted treatment viewed by most people as clearly beneficial or, alternatively, a patient may insist on aggressive therapy when most professionals consider the intervention futile. Simply because we do not agree with the decision, however, does not make it unwise from the perspective of the patient or the surrogate decision maker.

PROGRESS BEING MADE, MORE NEEDED

As reported in an article in the September 7, 2010, issue of *The New York Times*, a growing number of hospitals across the country are going beyond simply hiring interpreters and offering translated forms to help cross multicultural barriers. New York City's Elmhurst

Hospital Center, located in a borough where there are people from more than 100 countries and where 56 percent of the residents are foreign-born, was profiled as an institution that is particularly effective in designing programs and services to accommodate its diverse patient population.

Lactation consultants have become sensitized to the perceptions of Bangladeshi women; female obstetricians are on duty overnight in case a Muslim woman arrives in labor and does not want to be treated by a male doctor; and diabetes nutrition classes, where participants are mostly from Latin America, were modified after the educator acquired new insights about the diets of her Latino patients.

The impressive efforts of hospitals in Iowa, Pennsylvania, Texas and California were also cited. Coincidentally, another New York City hospital, Queen's Hospital Center, was awarded a Citation of Merit in 2010 by the AHA-McKesson Quest for Quality Prize Committee for its outstanding achievements in community involvement and outreach and overall commitment to equity. Although exemplary programs do exist, the reality of staffing constraints must be acknowledged. It would be wonderful to always have a female obstetrician on call to address the needs of Muslim women, but what if your hospital's call group is composed of three men and one woman? Physician recruitment plans should consider such issues.

Cultural, moral and social judgments, whether consciously or unconsciously made by healthcare professionals, certainly affect what is said to patients and their families and inevitably influence how they are treated. The more we understand how these judgments complicate and potentially interfere with optimal patient care, the more likely we can make more rapid progress in improving outcomes aligned with patient and family preferences.

Originally published in the January/February 2011 issue of *Healthcare Executive* magazine.

Discussion Questions

If the solution of "transparent confirmation" had not been suggested and implemented, what alternative would you recommend to address the dilemma presented by this case?

Given that the nation is becoming increasingly racially and ethnically diverse, what more can hospitals do to accommodate patients' preferences?

Transitioning to "Perfected" Informed Consent

William A. Nelson, PhD, HFACHE,
and Kate Clay, RN

FOR HEALTHCARE PROVIDERS AND patients to mutually understand and agree to the goals of care in a manner that is more ethically
sound will require transitioning to "perfected" informed consent
from traditional informed consent.

Before we explain what perfected informed consent is, it is important to first define what informed consent is.

The concept of informed consent is intended to promote the
patient's understanding and agreement with a physician's recommendation, but also allows patients the opportunity to refuse unwanted
interventions. Therefore, the concept should be understood as both
informed consent and refusal.

The ethical principle of autonomy is embodied in the process of
valid consent and refusal. The process seeks to support and respect
patients' self-determination in relationship to their values and healthcare goals. In order to be considered valid, consent must fulfill several
required elements:

- Adequate information: Healthcare providers must
  provide all necessary information regarding the nature
  of the recommended intervention, including its benefits
  and risks. Informed consent also requires disclosing the
  benefits and risks of all reasonable alternative interventions
  and no intervention at all.

- Decisional capacity: The patient must have decisional capacity, which is similar to the legal term *competence*. When patients lack competence or decisional capacity, the authorized surrogate should be identified and given the opportunity to represent the patient's wishes.
- Voluntary agreement: The patient's (or surrogate's) decision must be free of coercion and any undue manipulation that might undermine the voluntary nature of the decision.
- Documentation: For many procedures and treatments a signed consent form is legally or organizationally required as proof that consent occurred.

INFORMED CONSENT CONCERNS

The issue surrounding traditional informed consent is that some clinicians undervalue the consent process or see it as a legal or organizational nuisance, while others suggest that patients rarely understand the medical context, ultimately placing the decision back in the hands of the physician. The language used by clinicians when speaking to a patient, or in written form, can be incomprehensible to patients. In addition, clinicians may overestimate the benefits of a treatment or procedure and underestimate the risks or harms when communicating with a patient. And patients often sign the consent form without reading it, which then becomes useful only as documentation of signatures, rather than as the culmination of a dialogue incorporating the patient's understanding, preferences and goals of care into the conversation.

"PERFECTED" INFORMED CONSENT

Shared decision making supports patient informed choice, which leads to perfected informed consent, especially in those situations requiring signature consents. The term "perfected informed consent" was propagated by Benjamin Moulton, JD, senior legal advisor at the Foundation for Informed Medical Decision Making, in a 2006 article in the *American Journal of Law & Medicine.*

In the article, Moulton and co-author Jaime Staples King explained that perfected informed consent results when shared decision-making processes and tools are employed in place of the current consent process. The shared decision-making communication process between the physician and patient uses unbiased and complete information regarding all treatment options and information from the patient on personal factors that might make one treatment alternative more preferable than others. This open, two-way exchange of information and opinions about options, risks, benefits and values leads to better understanding and decisions about clinical management that is the foundation of the shared decision-making approach.

This approach is a conversation between two experts: the physician and the patient. The physician presents all known treatment options and their associated benefits and risks. The patient, who must live with the consequences of the benefits and risks, contributes her expertise in which she communicates her goals of care, including what she hopes to achieve, what aspects of each choice matter most, and what quality and quantity of life is desired. The final step is to ensure she has the financial means and social support necessary to implement the choice.

Such robust communication fosters informed choice: the choice a patient makes with a clinician, based on evidentiary and balanced information—including a discussion in language the patient understands—and elicitation of the patient's values (what matters most to the patient) with regard to the risks and benefits.

IMPORTANCE OF THE TRANSITION

The central reason for the transition is that healthcare executives and clinicians should want patients to understand what they are consenting to and provide the options they want. Current consent forms too frequently exist as proof of patient agreement for use in malpractice cases. The perfected informed consent process is both ethical and practical. This documentation differs from usual practice by detailing the content of the shared decision-making process. If a decision aid, such as a website, video or paper-based patient decision support tool was given to the patient, its content becomes evidence of what information the patient has been given. In the absence of a decision aid, if the clinician documented the options, risks and benefits, patient's stated values and preferences, and confirmation of the choice that the clinician and patient are agreeing to, the evidence is far more useful than the typical consent form in current use.

FOSTERING SHARED DECISION MAKING

There are several practical strategies healthcare organizations can employ to foster shared decision making, including:

- *Implement shared decision-making training.* Teach your clinicians the language and skills to have a meaningful conversation.
- *Integrate decision support tools for clinicians.* Clinicians cannot be expected to remember all the information about every condition. Support tools in the exam room assist with the options-risks-benefits conversation.
- *Incorporate decision support tools for patients.* When patients are provided with decision aids prior to the clinical encounter, they are better prepared to have an enhanced conversation with the clinician.
- *Redesign consent forms.* Incorporate patient-specific data and improve health literacy through a clear presentation of risk and benefit probabilities for the various options.

Acting in the patient's best interest respects autonomy. Only the patient knows specifically what is in his or her best interest. Therefore, clinicians should promote patient self-determination by adequately taking into account patient preferences. Many treatments have significant trade-offs, requiring patients to fully appreciate and understand the risks and benefits of their options prior to making a decision. The best vehicle for promoting patient autonomy is through a shift to a collaborative, shared decision-making process when deciding on a treatment plan.

Originally published in the July/August 2011 issue of *Healthcare Executive* magazine.

Discussion Questions

Shared decision-making supports informed patient choice. Describe how shared decision-making is different from the traditional understanding of informed consent.

Describe various approaches to implement shared decision-making in clinical care.

Patient-Centered Care: Rhetoric or Reality?

Paul B. Hofmann, DrPH, LFACHE

DURING A SERIES OF emails and an extended phone conversation, a young ACHE affiliate wanted to explore a recent column I wrote on culture clashes and moral judgments (*Healthcare Executive*, January/February 2011). She was specifically interested in developing a better sense of why healthcare employees and physicians are so frequently misunderstood by patients and their families and what can be done to improve the situation.

Certainly no employee or physician intentionally uses technical terminology or jargon to complicate the communication process when patients and their families are feeling particularly fragile and dependent. But this happens repeatedly. In addition, those who work daily in hospitals and clinics sometimes forget that our facilities can be very intimidating and confusing to people who want to be responsive to questions from staff members but concurrently are often reluctant to ask their own questions. The rush of activity, not wanting to appear unintelligent and a reluctance to do or say anything that might delay diagnostic or therapeutic interventions conspire to inhibit productive and meaningful conversations.

Adding to the challenge are the difficulties encountered by the growing proportion of patients whose first language is not English. This year The Joint Commission is stipulating that hospitals effectively communicate with patients when providing care, treatment and services. Surveyors are checking to confirm that the patient's race, ethnicity and preferred language for discussing healthcare have been documented in the medical record.

In addition, with shorter outpatient visits and lengths of hospital stays, the opportunities for intensive patient education are increasingly limited. The related financial and nonfinancial consequences for noncompliance by patients with discharge instructions are predictably multiplied under these circumstances.

BASIC ELEMENTS OF PATIENT-CENTERED CARE

When hospitals apply for the American Hospital Association–McKesson Quest for Quality Prize, candidates are partially judged on evidence demonstrating 14 elements of care representing genuine sensitivity to patients and their families. The elements are:

- Provides each patient the opportunity to define who is part of his or her family
- Engages patients and their families, to the extent they desire, in healthcare discussions and decisions
- Incorporates preferences and values of patients into decisions regarding their current and future healthcare needs
- Supports patient and family involvement in all aspects of patient care through ongoing two-way communication and encourages patients and family members to ask questions about their care and treatment to identify safety hazards
- Anticipates and meets the special needs of patients and families relative to their physical, psychological, developmental, cultural, spiritual and economic requirements while ensuring that all patients receive the same standard of care

- Provides patients and families with information and educational materials relative to their health needs and all hospital consent forms requiring the patient's (or duly designated proxy's) signature in a language they understand and at a level they are able to comprehend, and periodically evaluates adequacy and appropriateness of this information
- Ensures that all individuals who have knowledge of or direct access to patient information demonstrate an ongoing respect for each patient's privacy, decisions relative to patient care and individual values
- Evaluates patient experience of care and systematically addresses needed improvements
- Implements safeguards to preserve patient confidentiality without compromising communication between caregivers and patients and their families or impairing the coordination and continuity of care
- Ensures that patients' medical records are readily and continually accessible to them
- Offers patients, family members and visitors an easily accessible system for reporting safety and risk concerns
- Engages patients and families in defining quality healthcare and designing and improving workflow processes
- Creates opportunities for patients and families to serve on hospital advisory and management committees, including environmental design, to assist in the design and development of organizational policies and procedures, and to participate in staff orientation and continuing education
- Provides a physical environment that is welcoming, enhances access to information, and encourages participation by patients in their healthcare

Ideally, the above elements are intrinsic to an organization's culture and are not simply taken for granted. Solicited and unsolicited comments from patients and their families, donations, complaints, malpractice claims and Hospital Consumer Assessment of Healthcare Providers and Systems (HCAHPS) scores are among the many proxies reflecting how well an institution is doing in this critical area.

THE INCONSISTENCY OF INFORMED CONSENT

Regrettably, informed consent is an example of those issues that are too rarely recognized as legitimate litmus tests of patient-centered care. Four criteria must be met to obtain informed consent:

1. Patient competency is evident—the patient or his/her surrogate is mentally competent and has decision-making capacity
2. A comprehensive description of the invasive procedure, associated risks and benefits, and alternatives is provided to the patient
3. The decision is voluntary and free of any coercion
4. All the information is understood by the decision maker

Not surprisingly, each component of the informed consent process can be and frequently is inadequately addressed. When such is the case, the provision of patient-centered care may be irreversibly compromised.

If a patient agrees with the physician's recommendation, decision-making capacity is usually not considered a concern from the physician's perspective. During a description of the procedure, some physicians may omit a summary of their own limited experience and related clinical outcomes associated with the procedure. Further, physician and operating room availability can pressure a quick clinical decision when a more conservative approach may be appropriate. Even if these issues are not factors, it is still relatively uncommon for a physician to ask the patient to summarize his or her understanding of the procedure, potential complications and options—the most obvious way to confirm a patient's comprehension.

MODEST RECOMMENDATIONS

Just as the pursuit of quality is a never-ending journey requiring constant vigilance, so is achieving patient-centered care. None of the following recommendations can be fulfilled without the direct and conscientious commitment of senior leadership. Healthcare organizations should ensure that:

- There is absolute congruency between the organization's decisions, actions and behavior on the one hand and its vision, mission and values on the other; reality mirrors the institution's rhetoric
- Board, management, medical staff members and all caregivers, without exception, believe, support and exhibit the values
- Employees, physicians and volunteers are recruited with an explicit understanding that performance standards are nonnegotiable
- Orientation and continuing education programs reinforce the organization's expectations
- Special attention is devoted to supporting nurses who are frequently considered by patients and their families to be the most important, most accessible and least intimidating communicators
- Interdisciplinary rounding with patients and families is promoted to provide frequent opportunities to discuss and resolve issues and concerns

- Strong emphasis is placed on effective discharge planning and education to ensure patients and families understand the content, which helps prevent unnecessary readmissions
- All components of patient billing are clear, accurate and easily understood
- Regular performance reviews of all employees, including the CEO, include a specific measure, objective or goal that recognizes at least a portion of any compensation adjustment will depend on the individual providing tangible evidence of having contributed to improved patient-centered care
- The CEO routinely makes patient rounds and interacts with patients and their families, avoiding the rationalization that there is insufficient time to perform this essential activity on a regular basis

Patients should expect they will be treated as if they were part of the staff members' own families. Taking this approach and showing empathy, compassion and emotional support will reduce the prevalence of misunderstanding that frustrates not only patients and families but also staff members.

Originally published in the September/October 2011 issue of *Healthcare Executive* magazine.

Discussion Questions

Of the fourteen elements of patient-centered care, select seven you believe are most important and describe the rationale for your choices.

The author recommends ten steps hospitals should take to ensure patient-centered care. Which three do you believe will have the most impact, and why?

The Ethics of Avoiding Nonbeneficial Healthcare

William A. Nelson, PhD, HFACHE

ONE OF THE MOST vexing ethical challenges for healthcare executives focuses on the allocation of resources. ACHE's annual "Top Issues Confronting Hospitals" CEO survey has ranked "financial challenges" as a top concern for the last eight years. Because resources are finite—despite significant demand—an executive or a group of professionals within the organization must be able to answer the question, "How should limited resources be distributed?" As well as the parallel question, "How can organizations contain costs?"

Ethicists have offered different rationales for the basis of allocating limited resources by applying various understandings of distributive justice. Such discussions often focus on what comprises a patient's fair share of healthcare resources. This communitarian approach can run counter to the physician's fiduciary commitment to provide every individual patient with any needed and appropriate care.

The long-standing assumption underlying all debates about resource allocation is that resources are limited, so rationing of beneficial care is inevitable. In a 2012 article in the *New England Journal of Medicine (NEJM)*, "From an Ethics of Rationing to an Ethics of Waste Avoidance," Howard Brody, MD, a family physician and ethicist, argues that we ought to review this line of thinking in order to focus on the ethical responsibility of waste avoidance—that is, the avoidance of nonbeneficial care.

Brody draws attention to the need for physicians to recognize the ethics of waste avoidance as an important counter approach to the challenges associated with the allocation of resources. He correctly shifts the focus from denying care to the inappropriate use of medical resources—the abuse of which leads to a high level of spending and prompts the need for rationed care.

The need for avoiding waste, or nonbeneficial care, cannot be exaggerated. Donald M. Berwick, MD, and Andrew D. Hackbarth have indicated in their article "Eliminating Waste in U.S. Health Care" (*Journal of the American Medical Association [JAMA]*, 2012) that estimates suggest up to one-third of all health spending is wasted. That number represents not only some low-hanging fruit but a major portion of healthcare spending.

The failure to achieve value for money spent in the delivery of care in today's healthcare organizations is not only an economic misuse of resources, but an ethical failure. The avoidance of nonbeneficial interventions calls for a moral imperative to recognize, address and put an end to the misallocation of resources.

The application of nonbeneficial interventions runs contrary to health organizations' basic values in two fundamental ways. First, by wasting financial resources—providing services at high costs with little to no unit of benefit delivered—an organization undermines its own obligation to efficiency and fairness. Secondly, a physician's patient care commitment and the organization's values mandate that healthcare professionals only act in the patient's interest and avoid harm. Offering nonbeneficial interventions can mislead patients, and when accepted can cause complications, producing false positives that can take clinicians down a path of further and unnecessary actions.

Brody makes a noteworthy connection between avoiding interventions that do not benefit patients and the ethics surrounding medical futility. Medical futility is frequently discussed within the context of patients or family members demanding interventions that physicians know to be nonbeneficial based on empirical data. Thus, performing an intervention that is futile based solely on the patient's demand would violate the physician's integrity to act only in the patient's best interest. Similarly, would it not violate the basic tenets of professionalism for physicians to offer and provide a treatment that is inappropriate, based on either economic self-interest or poor evidence?

Because their recommendations to patients drive healthcare expenditures, physicians will need to play a major role in reducing the incidence of inappropriate interventions. As noted by Christine K. Cassel, MD, and James A. Guest, JD, in "Choosing Wisely" (*JAMA*, 2012), "physicians do not always have the most current effectiveness data, and despite acting in good faith, they can recommend diagnostic or therapeutic interventions that are no longer considered essential."

The authors also emphasize that physicians could benefit from improved communication skills when discussing intervention issues with patients, especially regarding interventions that yield limited or marginal benefits. The application of shared decision making, including the use of current decision tools, can assist in the deliberative process.

ADDRESSING OVERTREATMENT

In order to address the imperative to reduce waste in spending and promote robust two-way conversations between physicians and patients, many medical specialty societies have joined with the American Board of Internal Medicine and *Consumer Reports*, the nonprofit consumer organization, to foster the Choosing Wisely campaign (www.choosingwisely.org). As Cassel and Guest denote, many specialty groups in this growing campaign have developed lists of five treatments and tests that are regularly used in that specialty and which should be reevaluated by both patients and physicians.

The concept of developing the specialty "list of five" grew out of a proposal by Howard Brody in "Medicine's Ethical Responsibility for Health Care Reform—The Top Five List" (*NEJM*, 2010) to "restrict ourselves to the most egregious causes of waste . . . [so] we are genuinely protecting patients' interests and not simply rationing healthcare."

Examples of the treatments and tests on the lists of five include: the unnecessary use of CT scans and other imaging procedures for uncomplicated headaches; antibiotics for mild sinus infections; and X-rays, CT scans or MRIs for lower back pain. The various professional societies indicate that their lists do allow for potential exceptions—such as the use of imaging for lower back pain—when the physician suspects a serious underlying condition or when the pain has not lessened in six weeks.

The origins of the Choosing Wisely campaign are not only economically driven. Yes, there is an economic benefit in reducing waste, but the real driver for such a movement is ethical. The campaign reaffirms the professional commitment to social justice by acting in the patient's best interest, avoiding harm and promoting the cost-effective allocation of limited resources and true patient autonomy by providing an accurate understanding of the limited benefits of such interventions.

The Choosing Wisely effort has centered not only on actions taken by physicians but also on patients, empowering them with greater knowledge of healthcare treatments. This effort results in a more honest dialogue between patients and physicians of the potential benefits and harms of various interventions. To foster enhanced communication within the physician–patient relationship, *Consumer Reports* is disseminating consumer-friendly adaptations of the various medical specialty lists.

LEADERS' ROLE

The ethically grounded drive to reduce nonbeneficial healthcare should be expanded beyond the role of physicians and patients: Executives and the organizational context must also play a vital role. Because the delivery of healthcare services occurs within the context of an organizational structure and system for the delivery of care, executives should be aware of existing practice patterns in relation to professional standards. This point seems obvious; however, too often one reads a headline: "Hospital Chain's Inquiry Cited Unneeded Treatment . . . Excessive and Risky." Or one reads of CEOs presented with practice pattern data regarding extreme variations in the use of interventions, such as at end of life, and they seem surprised and unaware of what is occurring in their own facility.

Executives, in collaboration with other healthcare leaders, should ensure adherence to clinical practice guidelines suggested by the Choosing Wisely campaign. No longer can executives be unaware of deviation from clinical practice standards. System-oriented strategies are needed to ensure executives can be confident ethically grounded care is consistently delivered, such as:

- Establishing local clinical practice guidelines based on the specialty society criteria
- Developing methods for documenting and monitoring the implementation of practice guidelines
- Reviewing outcome measurement data and providing feedback to clinicians
- Facilitating shared decision-making education, including the use of decision tools
- Developing, monitoring and reporting the clinical application of shared decision making
- Creating a mechanism and procedure by which health professionals can discuss actions that potentially contribute to waste without retribution

The moral obligation to avoid nonbeneficial interventions cannot be clearer. What is less clear is how it will be achieved. Further empirical research will aid physicians regarding what is truly beneficial care, however—as indicated in the Choosing Wisely movement—there is sufficient data today to guide physicians.

Through outreach, such as the *Consumer Reports* efforts, there can be improved physician–patient communication, but the moral obligation is not limited to clinicians and patients. Executives need to join the movement, despite economic pressures, and ensure systems are in place in their organization to provide only beneficial care—thus achieving real alignment between the organization's mission and values and professionalism.

Originally published in the November/December 2012 issue of *Healthcare Executive* magazine.

Discussion Questions

Provide examples of common, recurring nonbeneficial treatments that are routinely offered to patients.

Discuss why clinicians have such a difficult task in avoiding nonbeneficial healthcare.

Ethics in Clinical Research

Richard A. Culbertson, PhD

CLINICAL RESEARCH IS NO longer the exclusive domain of the academic health sciences center but has extended into the everyday world of the healthcare executive in a wide range of organizational and clinical settings. This trend is a beneficial one in many respects, for clinical research is the R&D of the healthcare world in applying and validating discoveries from the realm of basic science (the bench) to the care of the patient (the bedside). Healthcare organizations have engaged in clinical research at a variety of levels as direct sponsors of research investigators or as part of a broader research network engaged in the conduct of clinical trials.

Total spending on health-related research and development from public and private sources in the United States reached $49.3 billion annually by 2010, according to ACHE's *Key Industry Facts: 2012*. This source of opportunity to advance the research dimension of one's organizational mission while opening new sources of revenue in a world of diminishing resources has proven attractive to clinicians in private practice settings and to community institutions, attracting new entrants to clinical research.

Ethical issues have always had a prominent place in discussion of clinical research. The ethical imperative of "first do no harm" has been violated by some studies in the past such as the infamous Tuskegee syphilis experiment begun in 1932 in which participants were not informed of the nature of the study and in which therapy for treatment of the disease was withheld. In response to public outrage, the study was terminated in 1972, and a formal presidential apology by President Clinton on behalf of the nation followed in 1997. Within the conduct of the study, informed consent by the participants was impossible because the study's objectives and a detailed explanation of relative risks and benefits (if any) of participation had not been disclosed to them.

The Belmont Report of 1979, which was prompted in part by the Tuskegee incident, led to the adoption of recommendations to avert future ethical lapses in clinical research as official U.S. Department of Health, Education and Welfare policy. These policy directives were based on specific ethical principles and were directed primarily toward protection of participants. The directives were specifically applied through policies of informed consent, assessment of risks and benefits, and responsible selection of study participants.

The ethical principle that most prominently figured in the Belmont Report was that of respect for persons. This premise has been a driving force in contemporary bioethics and is defined as the obligation of the organization and the executive to protect and preserve individual autonomy (self-determination) of participants in clinical research studies. In this regard, it parallels the drive toward protection of patient self-determination in the clinical setting that is embodied in ACHE's *Code of Ethics.* According to the code, the healthcare executive commits to "work to provide a process that ensures the autonomy and self-determination of patients or others served."

PROTECTION OF SUBJECTS

Federal regulation for protection of clinical trial volunteers in federally sponsored research projects has been highly developed through the Institutional Review Board mechanism of the U.S. Department of Health and Human Services. Many healthcare executives are part of organizations sponsoring their own IRBs or are members of research networks that assume IRB responsibilities. In the work of IRBs, the attainment of participants' informed consent is a central value, much as informed consent is essential to patient safety and self-determination in the clinical setting.

In their 2002 "Clinical Trial Volunteer's Bill of Rights," Kenneth Getz and Deborah Borfitz summarize the gist of these regulations for protection of subjects. Key elements involve informing the participant of the purpose of the clinical trial; all risks, side effects or discomforts that might be reasonably expected; and any expected benefits. The participant must be told what will happen in the study and whether interventions such as drugs and devices differ from those used in standard medical treatment. Available options should be discussed and assessed as better or worse than being a participant.

Throughout the clinical trial process, prevention of coercion, which diminishes patient freedom and detracts from the *respect for persons* tenet, is essential. The participant is to be allowed to ask questions about the trial prior to giving consent and at any time during the trial. She or he must have ample time to decide to consent free of pressure. The participant may refuse to participate for any reason before and after the trial has commenced and must be told of any medical treatments available if complications occur. All of the above provisions must be addressed in an informed consent form that is signed, dated and given to the participant.

Protection of study participants has proven crucial in gaining the public's confidence regarding the integrity of research studies and the absence of exploitation of their essential participants. This protection is especially necessary in the successful involvement of minority and underserved populations in studies. The literature demonstrates that variation in success of treatments exists across these lines and that generalizable results cannot be attained without the voluntary involvement of these individuals. In this regard, the ethical obligation of the executive in the conduct of clinical research is again no different than in the therapeutic setting.

CONFLICTS OF INTEREST

With the increasing fiscal attractiveness of clinical research has come an intensified focus on the obligation to minimize conflicts of interest—on the part of researchers and their organizations—resulting from financial interests that could affect the design, conduct or reporting of research results. In his 2011 book *Ethics in Health Services Management*, Kurt Darr defines conflict of interest as "a duality of competing interest when duties are owed to two or more persons or organizations and meeting the duty to one makes it impossible to fulfill the duty to the other."

Further, without full disclosure of conflicts to participants, the respect for persons principle is undermined, as the participant is giving consent based on incomplete information. Just as the American Medical Association's *Code of Medical Ethics* mandates that if a conflict develops between a physician's financial interest and the interest of the patient that the conflict must be resolved to the benefit of the patient (Standard 8.03), so must a conflict in the research world be resolved in favor of the public.

The National Institutes of Health promulgated regulations in 2011 to provide added barriers to conflicts of interest through investigator disclosure and formal institutional review. This intensified interest on the part of NIH requires certification of all investigators to meet stringent financial conflict of interest requirements. This was in part prompted by public revelations highlighted in the media of investigators profiting from the distortion of clinical trial results for the benefit of commercial interests from which they stand to profit.

Also of interest is the improper provision of information regarding the probable outcome of trials to investors who will profit if a drug or device can be successfully marketed. Significant interest is considered to be compensation or equity interest exceeding $5,000, intellectual property rights and reimbursed travel to a researcher by a sponsoring entity.

For healthcare executives, clinical research is a new but vital mission essential to the financial and social vitality of the organization and society in general. The ethical imperative for executives is to ensure research is conducted within policies that protect participants in research and that are for the good of the public.

Originally published in the May/June 2013 issue of *Healthcare Executive* magazine.

Discussion Questions

Do you think the clinical research safeguards described by the author to protect patients are sufficient? Why or why not?

All authors of research studies published in clinical journals are now required to disclose any possible conflicts of interest. Explain why such a requirement may or may not be adequate.

Necessary Competencies for Ethics Committees

William A. Nelson, PhD, HFACHE

ETHICS COMMITTEES ARE WIDELY accepted as an important resource for addressing ethical challenges in today's healthcare organizations. The value of ethics committees has been acknowledged by The Joint Commission, which established standards for an ethics mechanism to address ethical conflicts within healthcare institutions.

The traditional ethics committee tends to focus on ethics education, policy review and development and case consultation. Over the years, ethics committees have evolved to address not only clinical issues but also broader organizational issues such as conflicts of interest, allocation of resources, professional–personal boundaries and institutional marketing practices. As a result, ethics committees have the potential to be essential resources for not only clinicians and patients but also healthcare executives. Despite the presence of ethics committees in most healthcare facilities, and their potential for broad reach, they can be underused by executives.

WHY ARE ETHICS COMMITTEES UNDERUSED?

During educational programs, I frequently ask a series of questions to healthcare executive participants about their use of ethics committees. I begin by asking participants to raise their hands if they regularly encounter ethics issues. In response almost every hand in the audience shoots up. I then ask them if they ever feel uncertain about how best to address the ethics issues. Nearly the same number of hands is raised.

Next, I ask participants: Do you regularly seek out the ethics committee or some of its members to assist you in responding to ethics conflicts? In response to this question, very few, if any, hands are raised. Finally, I ask the participants: Do you encourage your clinical and administrative colleagues to seek out the ethics committee when they encounter ethics conflicts? Again, very few hands are raised. If I were to change the litany of questions to focus on legal issues and the use of risk management or legal counsel, would the responses be different? Probably.

When exploring the reasons why healthcare leaders rarely seek out their institutions' ethics committees or encourage others to use them, the responses vary dramatically. Some respondents believe that the ethics committee only addresses clinical issues and therefore would not be useful to leaders trying to address or reflect on organizational or business ethics issues.

But the most common response I hear from healthcare executives is they lack confidence in committee members. They do not feel committee members are sufficiently knowledgeable in organizational and managerial issues—the business and financial aspects of healthcare. Many leaders indicate that they wish committee members were better prepared to offer ethics-grounded thinking to the broader scope of issues encountered.

A task force of recognized ethics committee and ethics consultation leaders from throughout the U.S. recently published an important report on the core competencies for healthcare professionals performing ethics consultations. The task force's primary concern was quality assurance in the effectiveness of ethics consultations: Patients, families, surrogates and healthcare professionals should feel confident when they seek assistance regarding the ethical dimensions of healthcare. They should trust that the internal ethics consultants are competent and able to offer help.

A summary of the task force's report, written by Anita J. Tarzian and the American Society for Bioethics and Humanities' Core Competencies Update Task Force, was published in the February 2013 (Vol. 13, Issue 2) issue of the *American Journal of Bioethics*. The report can serve as a practical tool to ensure ethics consultants possess the needed knowledge and skills to be effective in addressing a wide range of issues, including organizational ethics challenges. When healthcare executives recognize and trust that their institutional ethics consultants possess these core competencies, it will build their confidence when seeking their assistance.

ETHICS CONSULTANT SKILLS AND KNOWLEDGE

The report notes that ethics consultants need to have specific knowledge and skills to accomplish two fundamental goals: the ability to identify and analyze the nature of the value conflict or uncertainty; and the ability to facilitate moral reasoning to provide an ethics-based resolution.

To effectively respond to ethics consultations, healthcare executives should feel confident that their facility's consultants have appropriate skills and knowledge. The report recommends three basic skills:

- **Assessment skills**—including the ability to identify and analyze the ethical uncertainty or conflict and to access and apply ethics knowledge from the organization's policies, professional guidelines or standards, and ethics literature
- **Process skills**—including the ability to facilitate a consult, communicate and document the consult, and collaborate with various professionals as part of the consult
- **Interpersonal skills**—including the ability to listen, ask questions and foster effective communication among the parties involved in a consult

In addition to these fundamental skills, ethics consultants should possess ethics-related knowledge. The report identified several core knowledge competencies including:

- **Moral reasoning related to ethics consultation**—basic ethical theories, principle-based reasoning, and theories of social and distributive justice
- **Basic ethics concepts and issues that are frequently encountered**—patient choice, conflicts of interest, confidentiality, end-of-life decision making and surrogate decision making
- **Clinical context**—awareness of the basic course of commonly seen illnesses, roles of various healthcare professionals and basic healthcare terminology
- **Organizational context**—mission and values statements, systems of care, organizational structures, medical record keeping, the role of executives and a basic understanding of healthcare financing
- **Organizational policies and procedures**—informed consent, advance directives, withholding and withdrawing life-sustaining treatment, human subject research, disclosure of medical errors and impaired professionals
- **Cultural beliefs of the population served**—racial, ethnic, religious and cultural groups, and the resources for addressing specific religious and cultural perspectives
- **Relevant professional codes of ethics and practice guidelines**—codes of ethics from all relevant professions (administration, medicine, nursing, etc.)
- **Applicable regulations and health law**—Joint Commission standards, end-of-life related laws, surrogate decision making and determination requirements, and organ donation and reporting requirements

The report makes the distinction between basic and advanced levels of the recommended knowledge and skills. The distinction is made because there is no one uniform manner in which ethics consultations are facilitated within healthcare institutions. Consultations can be performed by the committee as a whole, a small team (usually two to four consultants) or an individual committee member.

If the consultations are facilitated by the whole committee or a subcommittee, an advantage is that expertise can be pooled, whereas if a consultation is performed by a single person, that professional would need a more advanced level of expertise. Regardless of the institution's particular approach to consultation, appropriate additional resources should be identified. For example, if a case comes before the committee that involves a particular religious group (e.g., Jehovah's Witnesses) or a legal issue, the ethics consultants on call should be aware of the resources to which they have access to assist them in addressing those specific situations.

The task force report can assist committee members by acting as a self-assessment barometer, highlighting whether they are lacking any of the identified skills and knowledge areas. Any missing skill and knowledge areas can then become the focal point of an educational initiative. The educational initiative can be fostered through self-education, committee-wide education and/or attendance at formal healthcare ethics training programs and conferences. The American Society for Bioethics and Humanities created a useful education resource library to assist in these efforts.

The availability of effective ethics resources within a healthcare organization is critical for the successful handling of ethics issues. Competent resources should be available to assist and respond to both clinical and organizational ethics challenges. I often remind healthcare leaders that it is their responsibility to ensure that a capable ethics committee is present and properly resourced. Executives who feel less than confident about their ethics committees need to ask themselves the following questions: What am I doing to ensure that our ethics committee is a useful resource for all our employees and patients, and can I effectively respond to the ethical challenges faced?

Ethics committee members need executive leadership support to not only acknowledge the importance of an effective committee but also to provide adequate financial resources and time to attain the knowledge and skills needed to be a competent, valued and sought-after resource for addressing clinical and organizational ethics conflicts. The noted core competency report is a useful tool—for both executives and ethics committee members—for determining what is needed to foster assurance that your ethics committee and consultants have the appropriate knowledge and skills.

Originally published in the July/August 2013 issue of *Healthcare Executive* magazine.

Discussion Questions

Ethics committees are increasingly being used as an important resource for clinicians addressing ethical challenges. List some of the necessary knowledge and skills that ethics committee members should possess.

Describe which approaches should be implemented to ensure that ethics consultants are competent.

Balancing Issues of Medical Futility

William A. Nelson, PhD, HFACHE, and Robert C. Macauley, MD

THROUGHOUT MOST OF WESTERN medicine's history, paternalism reigned supreme. Physicians decided which treatments a patient would receive based on what they felt was in the patient's best interest. The patient wasn't informed of options the physician didn't believe were beneficial or appropriate, so the physician was never put in the position of refusing the patient's request for a specific treatment.

In the 20th century, however, medical treatments grew more advanced, physician judgment was no longer implicitly trusted and goals other than survival were recognized as worthy. Patient autonomy replaced beneficence as the preeminent ethical principle in medical decision making. Landmark statutes and court cases ushered in the era of autonomy, establishing the patient's right to refuse mechanical ventilation and other life-sustaining treatments.

Initially, patient autonomy was primarily manifested in the "right to die movement," in which patients refused potentially life-prolonging treatment because of concerns related to quality of life. Gradually, though, the notion of autonomy expanded to include requests for treatments that were ineffective, unproven or extremely expensive or for which the burdens would likely outweigh the benefits. Examples include CPR for a critically ill patient with metastatic cancer or tube feedings for a patient in a permanent vegetative state.

Such requests prompted the so-called futility movement of the 1990s during which physicians pushed back, claiming their own right to refuse (in this case, to provide treatments considered to be nonbeneficial). As the American Medical Association Code of Medical Ethics states, "Physicians are not ethically obligated to deliver care that, in their best professional judgment, will not have a reasonable chance of benefiting their patients. Patients should not be given treatments simply because they demand them." The conflict between the decision-making authority of a physician and a patient leaves us with a fundamental ethical question: Are there limits to patient or surrogate autonomy?

WHAT CONSTITUTES MEDICAL FUTILITY?

There are many understandings of the word *futility*. The word is derived from the Greek word futilis, meaning "leaky" or "worthless." The term comes from a myth in which the evil daughters of King Danaus are condemned to perpetually carry water in leaky sieves. Thus, an intervention is futile if it will not achieve its intended goal.

This is an important point because without knowing the intended medical goal, it's impossible to determine whether an intervention is futile. Consider a critically ill patient with an underlying lung disease who is unlikely to ever leave the hospital. If the patient's goal is to return home and lead an independent life, then intubation would be futile. However, if the patient's goal is to survive another day, then intubation may not be futile.

Once the patient's goal is identified, the next question involves the likelihood of achieving that goal. *Physiologic futility* refers to an intervention that has no chance of achieving the patient's goal. An example would be administering intravenous medications to stimulate the heart of a patient in cardiac arrest in the absence of chest compressions. Without those compressions to circulate blood, the medications will not reach the heart, and the intervention has no possibility of restoring spontaneous circulation.

More frequently, futility discussions involve therapies that could, conceivably, achieve the patient's goal. In other words, it's possible but highly unlikely. The problem here is determining the probability of success for a particular patient and whether that's enough to justify the treatment. This is where conflict often occurs, because a 1 percent chance of survival might seem very low to physicians, but to a family, it represents the patient's only chance for survival.

This debate over the appropriateness of goals extends to treatments with a high probability of success, such as medically administered nutrition and hydration in a patient who is in a permanent vegetative state. If the goal is to keep that patient alive, then that intervention will almost certainly achieve that goal. The question, then, isn't so much the likelihood of achieving the goal but whether the goal itself is worth achieving in relation to the patient's quality of life. This is known as *qualitative futility*.

ADDRESSING DISAGREEMENTS

The concept of medical futility is generally raised when there is a disagreement over the goals or benefits of treatment and when there is uncertainty regarding the appropriate resolution.

Medical futility disagreements can take up significant staff member time and effort, taint the experience of patients and their family members and potentially lead to litigation and negative perceptions on the part of the larger community. For these reasons, healthcare executives must ensure an organizational policy exists that provides clear and practical guidelines, including how to recognize situations of medical futility and a formal process for addressing futility disagreements.

To start, the organizational policy should indicate a general understanding of what is meant by medical futility. A helpful working definition is offered by James L. Bernat in a 2005 issue of the journal *Neurocritical Care*. It says medical futility occurs when patients or surrogates are requesting clinical interventions that are highly unlikely to result in any form of patient benefit, based on medical data and professional experience ("Medical Futility: Definition, Determination, and Disputes in Critical Care").

The next component of an organizational policy regarding medical futility is to provide practical guidelines for addressing futility disagreements when patients or their representatives request treatments deemed by healthcare professionals to be nonbeneficial. The first step is to identify the precise source of the disagreement followed by a concerted effort to resolve the disagreement.

Most situations can be resolved through a process of effective communication and dialogue. In some instances, the patient or his or her family members may not fully comprehend the diagnosis and prognosis. Factors such as language barriers, poor communication and medical literacy may impair transfer of information. Even after ensuring optimal communication, denial is a common response to being told a patient likely will not survive or regain his or her previous quality of life, especially if the change in the patient's condition is abrupt.

Personal issues such as guilt, intrafamily conflicts and self-interest may prompt family members to demand treatments that are known to be ineffective. And even if a family accepts the medical reality of the situation, faith in miracles may lead them to request ongoing support.

Often, identifying the source of the disagreement leads to its resolution, such as through improved communication, empathy and compassion. If thoughtful and culturally sensitive exploration of these issues does not yield resolution, other resources throughout the organization should be accessed. For example, seek assistance from the hospital's pastoral services team, ethics committee, palliative care team or patient and family advocates. Often the viewpoints of individuals from these departments can be helpful in aligning the patient, family members and medical team around a common goal.

If serious disagreement continues, consideration should be given to transferring care of the patient to another physician within the institution who might be willing to provide the requested treatment. If this is not possible, consideration should be given to transferring the patient to another institution whose approach to care would be more consonant with that of the family.

The process of optimized communication, emotional and cultural sensitivity, expert consultation and possible intra- or interinstitutional transfer will resolve most futility disagreements. There may, however, be situations in which the patient and family remain resolute in their demands and patient transfer is not possible.

Recognizing this, some institutions have authorized their institutional ethics committees in collaboration with organizational leadership and legal counsel to be arbiters of medical futility disagreements. If those ethics committees ultimately deem a requested treatment nonbeneficial, then after providing a time-limited reprieve to the family to make the transfer to another institution, the treating physicians are authorized to withdraw the nonbeneficial treatment.

A CRITICAL ISSUE IN TODAY'S HEALTHCARE ENVIRONMENT

Medical futility disagreements can be contentious, adversarial and protracted. But in an era of increasing healthcare costs—particularly in the last months of life—the questions of if, when and how institutions can ethically refuse requests for treatment considered to be nonbeneficial have returned to the forefront.

Patient autonomy remains a fundamental right but not an unlimited one. It must be balanced with the healthcare professional's obligation to only provide interventions that evidence indicates may benefit the patient in relation to care goals. And only through thoughtful communication and deliberation by way of a comprehensive and transparent policy can disagreements around whether a requested intervention would achieve these goals be resolved in an ethical, consistent and compassionate manner.

Originally published in the March/April 2015 issue of *Healthcare Executive* magazine.

Discussion Questions

Define the term *medical futility*.

Since medical futility frequently implies a disagreement between healthcare clinicians and patients or family members regarding treatment decisions, describe an effective approach for addressing such disagreements.

Making Ethical Decisions

William A. Nelson, PhD, HFACHE

NO ONE WOULD DENY clinical and administrative healthcare professionals regularly encounter ethical challenges. For clinicians, the challenges may relate to a conflict regarding withholding or withdrawing life-sustaining interventions or breaching patient confidentiality. For the executive, the conflict may involve a decision concerning a needed service that is a financial drain on the organization or the abusive behavior of a highly productive administrator.

What is the same for clinician and executive decision makers is the potential for an ethical conflict or controversy. All ethical conflicts are characterized by a number of common components. An ethical conflict occurs when an uncertainty, a question or a controversy arises regarding competing ethical principles, personal values, or organizational and professional ethical standards of practice. Examples of such standards include the American College of Physicians' *Ethics Manual* or the American College of Healthcare Executives' *Code of Ethics*.

Once an ethical conflict is identified, the challenge becomes how healthcare leaders and other staff involved in the situation should respond. The use of a systematic process can enhance the analysis leading to a response that is ethically justifiable. For the clinician, executive or ethics committee member, applying a systematic process can diminish the possibility of making quick decisions lacking thoughtful reflection and sound ethical reasoning.

THE IMPORTANCE OF A STANDARD
PROCESS FOR RESOLUTION

A little over a decade ago, I was changing positions. Because I talked frequently about the importance of systematic ethical reasoning, during a farewell gathering, I was given a small poster that hangs in my office today. It reads, "Ethics, schemethics; flip the damn coin." The cynicism serves as a constant reminder of the need for the opposite—to *always* apply a carefully developed process to address ethics conflicts. The process will take time and effort, yet it can lead to ethically defensible decisions rather than convey the general attitude, "Because I said so." The process can foster a focused application of ethical principles, institutional values and policies to ethical conflicts. It promotes thoughtful and, hopefully, respectful dialogue between the parties involved in the ethical conflict.

Unlike some decision-making models, the application of a uniform systematic process for addressing both clinical and administrative issues is a subtle-but-important distinction. It emphasizes that a process should not be based on such a distinction, in no small part because the distinction between clinical and administrative issues can be fuzzy, leading to challenging questions regarding which process is the most appropriate to follow in any given ethics situation. Therefore, using one process to address either type of conflict has clear benefits.

In a July/August 2005 *Healthcare Executive* column, "An Organizational Ethics Decision-Making Process," I described a process for facilitating systematic ethical reasoning in response to an ethical conflict. I still adhere to the basic elements of that process; however, after teaching and applying the process in practice, I recognize the need for refinements.

The following is an updated decision-making process for making ethical decisions.

Recognize the background (the circumstances leading to the ethics conflict). Identify all the relevant factors contributing to the ethical conflict. For a clinical case, it's important to understand the medical issues involved, such as the patient's diagnosis, prognosis, treatment options and goals of care. Additional key factors are the patient's preferences; personal values; decision-making capacity; and, when the patient lacks that capacity, determination of the appropriate decision maker. Each individual with a stake in the decision—the patient, the patient's family and staff members—should have an opportunity to express his or her perspectives regarding the various factors surrounding the ethical conflict. This discussion can take place during a group conference or in individual meetings. The importance of these discussions cannot be minimized to clarify the various perspectives. Additionally, understanding the relevant economic, policy, social and legal implications is essential. In this step, all the relevant factors from the perspective of all involved should be reviewed.

After identifying all the conflict-related factors, situations may arise in which it becomes clear the perceived ethical conflict is really a disagreement about the facts of the case. In exploring the factors giving rise to a clinical ethics conflict, such as with the nurses, patient, family and physicians, it can become obvious there are different interpretations of the facts. For example, in an end-of-life-care situation, the family may have a different understanding of the patient's prognosis than the physicians. This can be similar for organizational ethics situations. If the involved parties reach agreement concerning the facts, the ethical conflict may be diminished or even eliminated; however, in situations where the discussions reinforce that a conflict exists, the parties should move to the next step.

Identify the specific ethical question that need clarification. After determining all the facts, the various competing value perspectives and the contextual issues related to the ethical conflict, the next step is to specifically articulate the ethics conflict. Because these occur when competing values are at play, the ethical question should focus on identifying and agreeing on the competing values. For example, are healthcare professionals morally obligated to provide an intervention requested by the patient they deem to be nonbeneficial—the conflict focuses on the underlying issue of whether patient autonomy should be limited in any way? Ethical questions should be identified and reviewed in such a way that consensus is reached among all the relevant parties. Failing to identify the specific ethical conflict(s) creates significant barriers to achieving a clear response to that conflict.

Consider the related ethical principles and/or organizational values. The next step is to acknowledge the relevant ethical principles and/or the organization's values related to the ethical conflict. Do any particular organizational policies or, in some situations, legal perspectives, relate to the ethics question?

This step is an extension of the previous step—and in some situations, this step can be addressed at the same time as when the ethical question is identified. The precise order in this portion of the process is less important than ensuring that clear identification of the specific competing values is achieved.

Determine the options for response. In this step, the decision makers should recognize all the potential options for responding to the ethical question. This step includes reviewing the ethical justification for each option. What are the arguments for and against each option? Many people avoid this step or rarely look beyond the first suggested option. Such an approach can be attractive from a time perspective; however, it can lead to a decision lacking a critical analysis. Ethical decision making is more than following the steps in a quick, lock-step manner; it involves an appreciation for the complexity of each step and how each relates to the others.

Recommend a response. Following a thoughtful review of the various options and the ethical justification for each, decision makers should propose a response. One aspect for determining which option is morally justifiable is to assess the likely consequences of each option along with the underlying intention. This step is intended to prioritize the ethical principles or values related to each of the options. Ideally, consensus should be reached around the recommended option.

Once a recommended option is selected, it should be shared with all involved parties. The ethical justification should be included in the recommended course of action. For a clinical ethics case, the recommendation should be noted in the patient's chart or EHR.

Anticipate the ethical conflict. Unlike many decision-making models, this multiple-step process does not end with the resolution of the conflict response. I encourage this final step in the process—which, in some situations, may be the most challenging step in a systematic ethical-decision-making process.

Most ethical challenges focus not on isolated events, but on recurring issues. The presence of recurring ethical conflicts can undermine quality of care, staff morale, efficiency and productivity, operational costs and the organization's culture. Due to the recurring nature and impact of ethical conflicts, clinical and/or administrative staff—with assistance from the ethics committee and quality improvement program—should pursue an inquiry to determine how future conflicts can be prevented. To do so requires a thorough exploration of two fundamental questions:

- Why did the ethical conflict occur?
- What can be done to prevent the situation from recurring?

Exploring these questions can lead to a better understanding of how administrative and clinical leaders can develop strategies for anticipating and preventing similar conflicts before they escalate. This approach, as described in "Preventing Ethics Conflicts and

Improving Healthcare Quality Through System Redesign" (Nelson, W. A., et al., *Quality and Safety in Health Care*, 2010), features the application of methods and tools familiar to quality improvement. The process could lead to the development of ethics practice guidelines that can diminish the presence and impact of ethical conflicts throughout the organization.

FINAL THOUGHTS

Because no healthcare decision is made in a vacuum, ethical conflicts are best addressed when all the people who are legitimately involved have an opportunity to discuss their values, perceptions and concerns in an open and respectful environment.

Depending on the situation, greater or lesser attention may be required for a particular step in the process; however, no step should be ignored. The process is not an algorithm providing one clear answer to every ethical conflict, but rather it is a method for understanding different perspectives on the conflict and enhancing ethical reasoning. Just as ethical reasoning is not limited to the purview of healthcare ethicists or ethics committee members, the process can be applied by any healthcare professional when confronted with an ethical conflict.

Originally published in the July/August 2015 issue of *Healthcare Executive* magazine.

Discussion Questions

Discuss the importance of a knowing and applying a systematic process for addressing ethical conflicts.

The final step in the ethical decision-making six-step process is anticipating or preventing the ethical conflict. Why is this final step so important for today's healthcare organizations and clinicians?

The Urgent Need for Fatigue Management Policies

Paul B. Hofmann, DrPH, LFACHE

A NURSE STRIKES AND kills a cyclist—a father of two young children—while driving home from the hospital after working a double shift. Another healthcare professional falls asleep on the job in a group home; one of her patients dies after receiving insufficient oxygen.

These are two extreme, real-life examples bolstering growing evidence showing that when nurses, physicians and other members of the healthcare team are fatigued, they are more likely to jeopardize others or make a clinical mistake, regardless of their qualifications, compassion and dedication.

A 2013 report, commissioned by Kronos Inc. and conducted by HealthLeaders Media, indicated more than 25 percent of the nurses surveyed said fatigue caused them to make an error at work. The figure may actually be higher because many nurses, physicians and other staff members are likely unaware when fatigue affects their judgment.

Although the issue of healthcare provider work hours and sleep deprivation has been studied for years, healthcare has been slow to enforce policies addressing fatigue.

INCREASING EVIDENCE OF NEED FOR ACTION

In the November 2007 issue of The Joint Commission's *Journal on Quality and Patient Safety*, Steven Lockley, PhD, and his colleagues with the Harvard Work Hours, Health and Safety Group provided a comprehensive review of the effects of healthcare provider work hours and sleep deprivation on safety and performance. In its 2007 analysis, the Harvard Group determined that "long work hours increase the risk that nurses and doctors will suffer an occupational injury with potentially devastating long-term consequences and increase the risk of motor vehicle crashes."

They concluded the number of hours worked by U.S. healthcare providers is unsafe.

"To reduce the unacceptably high rate of preventable fatigue-related medical error and injuries among health care workers, the United States must establish and enforce safe work-hour limits," the authors wrote.

In 2010, teaching hospitals were required to place an 80-hour weekly limit on house staff; however, James Bagian, MD, director, healthcare engineering and patient safety, University of Michigan, said recently he is unaware of any institution that has an effective policy for residents and, in his experience, "The situation is worse for other care providers."

There is much more robust literature on fatigue management in other fields, particularly and predictably in ground and air transportation. For example, in its February 2012 issue, the American College of Occupational and Environmental Medicine's *Journal of Occupational & Environmental Medicine* contained detailed guidance on fatigue risk management.

The ACOEM report highlighted four points regarding the risk of employee fatigue in the 24/7 workplace:

- Fatigue is related to duration of sleep and timing of sleep.
- Inadequate sleep is correlated with a variety of adverse medical outcomes.
- Various shift work schedules can affect both the duration and timing of sleep.
- Inadequate duration of sleep is correlated with injury rates.

Last year, the American Organization of Nurse Executives reported 56 percent of survey respondents said their hospitals disregard required rest periods, and 65 percent said their hospitals do not have policies regarding cumulative days or extended shifts. One hospital with which I work has a 48-hour week work limit and another has a 60-hour limit. Undoubtedly, other hospitals have different limits, but how consistently are these restrictions monitored?

In addition to fatigue caused by too many hours of work at the hospital, it is increasingly common for hospital employees to have multiple jobs. Hospitals with policies stipulating a limit of 48 hours or 60 hours per week rarely, if ever, take this reality into consideration. Furthermore, in many urban areas where housing is more expensive, longer commutes are increasingly common. Research has verified that driving while tired, like driving under the influence of alcohol or drugs, results in slower reaction times and possible accidents.

As expected, studies also have confirmed sleep and the circadian system also play an important role in cardiovascular health. A 2015 study published in the *American Journal of Preventive Medicine* involving almost 75,000 U.S. registered nurses and 22 years of data concluded mortality from all causes appeared to be 23 percent higher for women with 15 years or more of rotating night shift work.

PREPARING A MEANINGFUL FATIGUE MANAGEMENT POLICY

It is both organizationally urgent and ethically essential that organizations take a stand on employee fatigue and create a fatigue management policy that promotes both patient and employee safety.

A logical first step in creating a policy is to engage a focus group of nurses and others to begin discussing the issue and solicit ideas and recommendations.

The policy should begin with a concise description of its purpose. By using this introduction to emphasize why the policy is needed, the hospital can explain that patients, staff and the community will benefit by having a clear statement of steps taken to prevent, or at least minimize, fatigue and its adverse outcomes.

The American Nurses Association, representing the interests of the nation's 3.1 million nurses, suggests this policy:

- Limit shift lengths to 12 hours and work weeks to 40 hours.
- Abolish mandatory overtime.
- Promote regular rest breaks.
- Allow nurses to decline assignments they think will cause fatigue.
- Restrict consecutive night shifts for nurses who work both days and nights.
- Provide nurses with places to sleep or transportation when they feel too tired to drive.

Expecting hospitals to limit the work week to 40 hours, given unpredictable changes in patient census and staffing resources, may be unrealistic, but this doesn't mean hospitals shouldn't review their current practices and establish an appropriate policy.

In assessing its safety culture and staff resilience, Duke University Hospital asks nurses to indicate how often they got less than five hours of sleep in the past week, a threshold below which social and emotional functioning are significantly compromised. Analyzing the data by clinical service unit and comparing changes between survey periods allows leaders to develop and focus their organization's intervention strategies and also helps predict where there are vulnerabilities (e.g., the potential for disruptive behavior and delays in the delivery of care resulting from nurse fatigue).

Just as adult children are hesitant to ask an elderly mother or father to give up their car keys, there are obvious difficulties in enforcing a policy when it may be evident an employee should not be working an extra shift or driving. It is quite likely the employee will reply, "I'm fine and have no problem working a double shift and driving home."

As emphasized in "The Myth of Comprehensive Policies" (*Healthcare Executive*, September/October 2012), even the best policies are meaningless if staff are not educated in their application, compliance is not monitored, areas of noncompliance are not addressed, and the policy is not periodically reviewed and revised to ensure its continued value.

Preventing even one tragedy affecting a patient, employee or member of the community is worth the investment.

Originally published in the September/October 2015 issue of *Healthcare Executive* magazine.

Discussion Questions

Given solid evidence that healthcare worker fatigue results in occupational injury, patient harm, and institutional liability exposure, why aren't more hospitals addressing this issue effectively?

If a supervisor or colleague is told by an obviously fatigued healthcare professional, "I'm OK," what options should be considered?

The Ethics of Big Data

Richard A. Culbertson, PhD

IN A SMALL-DATA WORLD of paper charts and limited electronic data storage, control of patient data was a much simpler undertaking. The healthcare executive could feel relatively secure that patient information could be maintained in relative confidence, although this cumbersome approach was not free of incursions. Today's world of big data presents added technical challenges of ensuring privacy as patient data is aggregated into larger databases for billing or quality assurance studies.

Big data has emerged as a constant in contemporary life that is viewed with both enthusiasm and trepidation. For the healthcare executive, the availability of big data has resulted in an array of ethical challenges unimaginable a decade ago. The questions these challenges present are not simply technical in nature, and they call into question some of the fundamental precepts of ethical decision making for the executive and the patients she or he serves.

Without question, the increased use of big data will affect patients, and it is vital that healthcare leaders ensure their organizations have safeguards in place that protect the confidentiality of the patients they serve. However, a companion responsibility to develop evidence-based clinical practices may be on a collision course with the emerging landscape that is being shaped by the use of big data in healthcare.

Before delving into the ethics of big data, it's important to first understand what big data is and how it's used for the benefit of patients and organizations. Big data is a collection of data sets so large and complex that it becomes difficult to process using on-hand database tools or traditional data-processing applications. The objective is to establish a correlation of observed phenomena gleaned from "massively parallel software running on tens, hundreds or thousands of servers," according to Adam Jacobs, PhD, senior software engineer at 1010data Inc.

The beneficence of big data for the patient and the healthcare organization can take two forms. One is scientific advancement in the form of identification of better treatments that can be established as superior through comparison across large population groups, to the ultimate benefit of all. The second is an economic one for the organization as data is increasingly monetized and purchased as a commodity.

BIG DATA'S HEALTH BEGINNINGS

The application of big data to healthcare that captured the attention of the public was the Google Flu Trends project of 2008. Based on two years of prior experience, Google researchers asserted that the spread of winter flu could be predicted nationally, down to specific regions and states. This was achieved through identification of 45 search terms related to flu and identifying correlations between millions of user flu-related searches and eventual flu-case reports to the Centers for Disease Control and Prevention.

The audacity of the Google claim was that the information was available one to two weeks ahead of the traditional case reports tabulated by the CDC. This led to examination of this method in subsequent flu seasons. Skepticism emerged in 2014 when researchers at Northeastern University, in conjunction with Harvard University's Institute for Quantitative Science, reported that Google Flu

Trends had significantly overestimated flu incidence rates from 2010 to 2013.

ONWARD WITH BIG DATA

The volume of patient specific clinical information has been greatly accelerated by the national movement to EHRs and the promise of comparability of massive amounts of clinical data in real time derived from previously unimaginable numbers of patients. In the face of this new resource, the unreliability of Google's efforts has not deterred others from attempting to employ big data analytics in advancing healthcare effectiveness.

For example, the Patient-Centered Outcomes Research Institute was established in 2010 to oversee the conduct of pragmatic clinical trials with information obtained from the health records of large numbers of patients—ideally, one million or more lives in a comparison network. Since its founding, PCORI has made substantial grants available to researchers for comparative effectiveness studies of various therapies such as use of aspirin in averting cardiac disease. Significant numbers of healthcare systems in turn have made the decision to join the PCORI-funded networks and make patient data available for study purposes.

The Health eHeart study at the University of California–San Francisco initiated in 2013 is an interesting example of a partnership of traditional academic researchers with private venture capitalists who fund the study. The study seeks 1 million participants globally to be followed through questionnaires and remote monitoring. Jeffrey Olgin, MD, a principal investigator on the team, has opined that "The Health eHeart study is opening up a whole new science" based on analyses of large populations versus small and expensive traditional clinical trials.

Scholars have identified the ethical dilemmas of this emerging world as informed consent, patient engagement, privacy and confidentiality, and data sharing. All of these concerns apply to the role of the healthcare executive in making ethical decisions in the face of increasing economic and scientific pressure and the admonition to "do no harm" as a prime responsibility.

A more difficult ethical challenge that big data poses is that analytic uses for this information may not yet have been devised. For example, a new approach to the treatment of rare cancers might be proposed that would require health information for millions of individuals to ensure sufficient patient analysis. How can consent be obtained given that treatments have already been employed? How can the principle of respect for persons be balanced against the beneficence for a broader population that might benefit from a more effective treatment?

Sacrificing privacy is still deplored in the health world. Obtaining consent as a key concept in the ethical value of respect for persons remains an obligation of the health executive, but consent is often unobtainable from persons in large data populations except through blanket consents that do not provide the specificity we now demand. The management of patient information in big data sets and the determination of what constitutes minimal risk to the patient in its use will ethically challenge healthcare executives for the foreseeable future.

When discussing and taking action on the ethical situations that may surface with big data, it's important to know the short- and long-term implications.

SHORT-TERM IMPLICATIONS

Many of our systems for patient consent are predicated on "small data" models, notably written information in a discrete physical patient chart. In this world, the healthcare executive is obliged to protect the content of patient information from viewers other than those authorized by the patient through the consent process. This obligation to protect patient information reflects the ethical principle of respect for persons, and it remains the ethical obligation of ACHE members as observed in the Ethical Policy Statement "Health Information Confidentiality."

The ACHE policy statement obligates the executive to "obtain written agreements that detail the obligations of confidentiality and security for individuals, third parties and agencies that receive medical records information, unless the circumstances warrant an exception." As the value of large data sets comprised of information from multiple individuals for commercial and medical research purposes becomes increasingly apparent, the number of requests for exception will inevitably increase. As venture capitalist Vinod Khosla has suggested, "Biological research will be important, but it feels like data science will do more for medicine than all the biological sciences combined."

LONG-TERM IMPLICATIONS

The ACHE Ethical Policy Statement "Health Information Confidentiality" obligates the executive to "participate in the public dialogue on confidentiality issues such as employer use of healthcare information, public health reporting, and appropriate uses and disclosures of information in health information exchanges." This dialogue will be increasingly complicated in a world in which leading ethicists disagree on the primacy of the respect for a person's principle and strict adherence to our traditional view of consent versus the beneficence that might result from the identification of superior forms of treatment for given disease states. It will be incumbent upon the executive to engage in the discussion of whether this constitutes an unjustifiable intrusion into patient privacy and the level of risk in pursuit of societal gain that could be considered minimal and thus justify waiver of current consent strictures.

Originally published in the November/December 2015 issue of *Healthcare Executive* magazine.

Discussion Questions

Given the ethical tension between preserving informed consent and confidentiality of patient information on one hand and capitalizing on the undeniable benefits of big data sets on the other, what ethical criteria might be used to make wise choices?

In view of healthcare executives' many priorities, what options could be pursued efficiently to influence this debate's outcome?

Patient's Plea—Look Closer, See Me

Paul B. Hofmann, DrPH, LFACHE

As MANY OF YOU know, I have authored this column for several years and am quite passionate about the topic. But what you may not be aware of is that I make ICU ethics rounds at two hospitals where I sit on their ethics committees. It is during rounding that I am reminded even more of the influential position we as healthcare executives are in to create and sustain an organizational culture that ensures patients are treated with respect.

The topic of rounding has been covered in this magazine many times, most notably in "Patient-Centered Care: Rhetoric or Reality?" (September/October 2011), in which most executives asserted they simply did not have enough time to conduct patient rounds, considering their full schedule of meetings and other commitments. I contended this was a convenient rationalization for deciding not to devote at least one hour three to five times a week to this activity because of "higher priorities."

Regular executive involvement with patients and families conveys an unambiguous signal to physicians and employees that senior executives genuinely care about patients, their families and the hospital experience by spending time with them. It was this point that Derek Feeley, PhD, president and CEO, Institute for Healthcare Improvement, Cambridge, Massachusetts, and an ACHE Member, conveyed during the IHI's Annual National Forum in 2016. He said that when we fail to treat patients with dignity and empathy, we are doing just as much harm to those we serve as if we were committing a physical medical error. He also urged attendees to understand that safety is more than just the avoidance of physical harm.

Leaders must be deeply committed to learning what is going on in the care process of their organization and then have the humility, clarity and courage to set in motion the changes to improve them. Many resources exist to help you achieve this aim. One in particular is an article I authored in the January/February 2006 issue of *Healthcare Executive*, "Becoming More Effective Patient Advocates," which is still relevant today.

PATIENTS AS INDIVIDUALS

In addition to traditional care-process resources, patient anecdotes are an effective means of reinforcing the importance of viewing patients as individuals. The following stories include reflections by a physician, an excerpt of a poem from an elderly patient to her nurse and comments on staff insensitivity by a professor. These are powerful illustrations of why we must recognize patients as unique individuals and focus *not only on who patients are but also on who they have been.*

A Physician's Lament

In the March 7, 2016, issue of *KevinMD Stories*, Edwin Acevedo Jr., MD, a surgical resident, vividly described his feelings when realizing a sobbing older man had just lost his wife. Acevedo acknowledged how he would never know her "when she dressed up for a ball, or how her husband had asked her to marry him, or how it felt to be part of their first family picture, or how it felt to buy their first house together, or how they ended every single day with a good night kiss."

His poignant description was a powerful reminder that staff members know the patient but usually not the person.

An Elderly Patient's Plea for Recognition

Over 40 years ago, I was fortunate to learn of an anonymous poem discovered among the belongings of a hospital patient who died in Scotland. It was titled "What Do You See?" and its message is just as relevant today as when it was written. The patient begins by asking, "What do you see, nurses, what do you see? What are you thinking when you're looking at me? A crabby old woman, not very wise, uncertain of habit, with faraway eyes?" Then, she eloquently reminds the nurses of why they should recall her as a child of 10, a young girl of 16, a bride at 20, a mother at 25 and a grandmother at 50.

She concludes by writing, "I remember the joys, I remember the pain, and I'm loving and living life all over again. I think of the years . . . all too few, gone too fast, and accept the stark fact that nothing can last. So open your eyes, nurses, open and see, not a crabby old woman, look closer . . . see ME!!"

Comments on Staff Insensitivity by a Professor

Invariably, when visiting a physician's office or observing hospital staff interacting with patients, I still sadly recall a college professor's letter to the editor of *The New England Journal of Medicine*, published in 1983. She expressed her discomfort about a common, and some might suggest unimportant, practice of calling patients by their first name. The last three paragraphs of her letter should be required reading for everyone who works in a hospital. She wrote:

> Being on the examining table or undergoing diagnostic procedures can be a scary business. It feels as though more than clothes have been stripped away; there is loss of confidence, of dignity, and of one's sense of individuality. As a patient, your name is one of the few unique descriptors left to you. It should be yours to 'give away' only if you wish. . . .

The issue may go far deeper than courtesy or dignity. The physician's role includes the task of enlisting the patient's own healing powers. Any procedure that increases confidence and inner energy will be important; any procedure that disempowers or diminishes the sense of self may impede the patient's progress. An insidious effect of the automatic use of the first name is to make the patient a child again. By reinforcing dependency and passivity, you have stolen power from your potential ally.

My plea to the medical community is to call patients by their full names until you can ascertain their preference. The skillful use of names can be a powerful instrument indeed, but you squander its effectiveness by the present practice.

CRITICAL LESSONS

If healthcare executives are uncertain about how to motivate staff to be more empathetic, they should read "A View From the Edge—Creating a Culture of Caring," authored by Rana L. A. Awdish, MD, in the January 5, 2017, issue of *The New England Journal of Medicine*. As the result of her own experience as a patient, she describes how new employees at Henry Ford Hospital, Detroit, where she specializes in pulmonary, critical care and internal medicine, are "taught to recognize different forms of suffering: avoidable and unavoidable."

When hospitals sometimes seem like institutional pressure cookers and lengths of stay continue to fall, it is understandable that physicians, nurses and other caregivers have minimal time to acquire meaningful insights about the individuals they are treating. This is particularly true for hospitalists who often have had no contact with their patients prior to hospitalization. In the January/February 2017 *Healthcare Executive* cover story, "The Care Continuum Universe: Delivering on the Promise," the author writes, "Many of us now know the most effective way to care for patents is when they are at the center of care, not the hospital or health system."

The article also highlighted Catholic Health Initiatives as one of three health systems delivering on the promise of the care continuum universe, stating that CHI "views the continuum of care as centered on the 'person'—as opposed to the 'patient.'"

It is regrettable that we must be reminded of this essential truth.

Originally published in the May/June 2017 issue of *Healthcare Executive* magazine.

Discussion Questions

Describe your views about why staff members should do their best to know the recipient of their care as both a patient and a person.

Beyond the author's recommendations, what additional steps might be taken to ensure that patient-centered care is also person-centered care?

Recording Devices Serve as Aid to Patients

William A. Nelson, PhD, HFACHE

JOE WAS SITTING IN the ED with a fractured rib from a bad fall when he began experiencing symptoms unrelated to his injury. After an examination, a physician informed Joe that he may be suffering from atrial fibrillation, or an irregular heartbeat. Following an EKG and a telephone cardiology consult, the physician told Joe it was fine to go home from the ED but that he needed to see a cardiologist soon for a more thorough evaluation.

Joe prepared himself for the cardiology appointment by researching atrial fibrillation and discussing this possible diagnosis with physician friends. He also prepared questions for the cardiologist, then asked his wife to join him for the visit, explaining that he wanted her to be a second set of ears—to hear what the cardiologist might tell him. Joe did not want to miss anything.

This real scenario is an example of how important it is to some patients to have a "second set of ears" to better hear and understand physician information regarding their healthcare issues. However, what if a patient lacks the opportunity to have another person monitor a consultation? Are there alternate or better approaches to ensuring that a patient understands what is communicated during a patient–clinician encounter?

MOTIVATING PATIENT RECORDING

An approach that has received increasing attention involves patients seeking to digitally record their clinical encounters. A study published in a 2015 issue of *BMJ Open* indicated that patients using recording devices in this manner can benefit from such an approach when referring to the recordings later.

The study explained that the primary reason patients recorded consultations was the desire to improve their understanding of what was being communicated during an encounter. Patients described how listening to the recording afterward served as an assessment of their understanding and helped them recollect what was said during the session. Because patient–clinician encounters can involve a good deal of information, these recordings can reassure patients that what they thought they heard was correct or otherwise clarify the information received. Patients also indicated that having the recording serves as a useful reference if they need to refer back to the information at a later time.

The patient can also share the recorded experience with others if the need to discuss the patient–clinician encounter arose. For example, if Joe's wife did not accompany him for the cardiology visit and he instead recorded the encounter, he could let her listen to the recording later to check if her understanding of what was communicated aligned with his. Sharing the discussion could be particularly beneficial if Joe's health issues were particularly complex and required challenging decision-making later.

Perhaps the best reason for recording encounters seems to reflect the concept driving much of current healthcare: patient-centered care. As the study in *BMJ Open* stated, "The prime benefit was that of empowerment . . . recording openly was viewed as a mechanism to focus the clinician's attention, to reduce the power imbalance and potentially reduce future need."

RESPONSE TO PATIENTS RECORDING CLINIC ENCOUNTERS

Other studies show that at some institutions the clinicians themselves offer recordings to patients and family members, particularly in oncology and pediatrics, where complex and emotional issues are discussed. Despite a few hospitals and clinicians endorsing this patient-centered care approach, however, the practice appears to be uncommon.

Many clinicians are most likely surprised when a patient seeks permission to record an encounter. In fact, clinicians' reactions may be less than enthusiastic to the idea of their patients recording their visits. Clinicians may insist that the patient explain why, with the clinician's response and questioning directly or indirectly reflecting concerns. They may wonder if the recordings could be used against them at some point, becoming a potential setup for litigation. Further, the presence of a recording device may raise concerns by clinicians and administrators regarding issues of ownership, confidentiality and privacy of the digitally collected information.

Many clinicians' concerns are likely to be anticipated by patients, so they may avoid asking the clinician's permission to record the conversation. Patients may fear that doing so could lead to negatively impacting the clinician–patient relationship or may even prompt denial of care. This has led some patients to covertly record encounters. In the world of smart phones and other digital recording techniques, covert recording is certainly possible.

Despite the concerns of clinicians and others, research has clearly suggested that patients benefit from recording office visits and other patient–clinician sessions. As a result, the empowering activity can foster patient-centered care and enhance informed patient choice.

In the August 8, 2017, *JAMA* article "Can Patients Make Recordings of Medical Encounters?" authors identified 33 studies of patients using audio recordings. According to the article, "Audio recordings were highly valued across the studies . . . reporting greater understanding and recall of medical information. . . . Clinicians and patients report benefits. In addition, liability insurers maintain that the presence of a recording can protect clinicians."

ROLE OF EXECUTIVES AND HEALTHCARE ORGANIZATIONS

Whether clinicians and organizations will allow patients to record encounters needs to be carefully considered and captured in healthcare organizational guidelines and policies. Undoubtedly some healthcare executives may be uncertain about whether recordings are appropriate, including their being a source of legal concerns. This uncertainty is not unreasonable. However, executive leaders should also avoid knee-jerk responses spurred by that uncertainty. There was a time when some leaders believed that informing patients of a medical error would inevitably lead to litigation, rather than recognizing the benefits of being an organization that is transparent and truthful with the population it served.

Healthcare leaders should facilitate thoughtful reflection on the issue of recording patient–clinician encounters. One key issue to address is the legality of recording medical encounters. In the 2017 *JAMA* article, the authors indicated that the issue has been made complex due to varying state laws. However, "39 of the 50 states conform to the single party consent rule" regarding the making of recordings; that is, only the consent of any one person is sufficient.

Organizations considering the issue should include a careful review of the relevant literature in addition to garnering ethical and legal counsel. Gaining patients' perspectives on the matter of recording is also essential for policy-making, as is exploring the experiences of hospitals that have implemented the approach.

In considering recording guidelines, leaders should contemplate whether a proactive approach to audio and even video recordings should be employed in some situations, rather than waiting for patients to ask if they can record their clinical conversations. A proactive approach could diminish situations where patients fear broaching the topic might trigger a negative response, driving them to then act covertly.

Along with a thoughtfully crafted recording policy that includes guidelines for clinicians and patients, a carefully planned educational thrust is necessary prior to the implementation of a policy.

In reflecting upon the acceptability of recording an encounter, one should not assume recording represents a breakdown of the traditional patient–provider relationship. Allowing patients to record communications with healthcare professionals can serve as a means to enhance the relationship. The recordings can be replayed to facilitate recall, increase understanding of information, share with others and promote informed patient choice in decision-making.

Just as Joe asked his wife to accompany him to his cardiologist appointment, patients who record clinical encounters can have a second set of ears, too.

Originally published in the March/April 2019 issue of *Healthcare Executive* magazine.

Discussion Questions

Research has demonstrated that a patient's recording of conversations with healthcare professionals can enhance patient understanding and compliance. Explain why some clinicians are reluctant to promote the use of recording devices.

Provide examples of how clinicians can incorporate the use of a recording device in patient care.

The Plight of the Incapacitated, Unrepresented Patient

Paul B. Hofmann, DrPH, LFACHE

CLINICIANS AND HOSPITALS INCREASINGLY find themselves in the challenging position of providing treatment to patients who do not have the ability to make their own medical decisions, nor have they designated surrogate decision makers. Given this is a difficult and growing concern, which has major ethical and resource implications, senior management should develop effective institutional strategies for helping clinicians optimize the management of these patients.

One of the most common reasons for an ethics consultation involves an incapacitated patient who is unrepresented, and the attending physician or a specialist needs to obtain time-sensitive informed consent for an invasive diagnostic or treatment procedure. The situation is complicated further when there is uncertainty or even disagreement among clinicians about the wisdom of proceeding with dialysis, a liver biopsy, surgery, inserting a percutaneous endoscopic gastrostomy tube, performing numerous other procedures requiring consent or writing a do not resuscitate order.

For many reasons, more patients are unable to make decisions on their own behalf and have no identified family member or friend to represent their best interests. Among these reasons are:

1. Despite efforts to raise the number of people who have completed advance directives, including their preferences

for end-of-life treatment options and the designation of a surrogate decision maker, less than 25 percent of Americans have them.

2. The fastest-growing population cohort is composed of people 65 and older who have chronic conditions and comorbidities, and those over 80 who are more likely to live in continuing care retirement settings, nursing homes or board-and-care facilities.

3. Regardless of age, a patient's capacity to make decisions is invariably influenced by trauma, physical illness, treatment, medication and mental health issues, including dementia.

4. Families are smaller, and often members live in other parts of the country with less contact with their relatives.

5. Many communities are struggling with a sizable number of homeless people who are more likely to have psychiatric disorders. These individuals frequently depend on hospital EDs for primary care, but they can be noncompliant and abusive. Placing such patients on involuntary holds when they risk inflicting harm to themselves or others may address an immediate need. However, such holds are time restrictive and do not establish a clear pathway for subsequent medical decisions consistent with the patient's best interests.

6. Family members and friends of homeless patients may be increasingly reluctant or unwilling to serve as the patient's representative when psychiatric and substance abuse issues are present.

7. The process for obtaining a conservator can be tedious and laborious, and many conservators are overextended. Consequently, significant delays in receiving a decision are common.

RECOMMENDATIONS

- Ask patients seen in the ED or admitted to the hospital for the name of at least one surrogate decision maker who can speak on their behalf should they become incapacitated.

- Recognize that although some unrepresented patients are homeless, they may have friends who have knowledge of their values and treatment preferences.

- Acknowledge that social workers, once described as the conscience of the hospital, are exceptionally creative detectives capable of locating relatives or friends who were thought to be nonexistent.

- Develop a policy and related procedures describing steps for locating a patient's relatives or friends. For example, people living alone in an apartment may have a neighbor or apartment manager who could be helpful. Gaining access to a patient's storage unit can produce critical contacts. A patient's cell phone or wallet are valuable sources of information. If known, the patient's current or previous primary care provider may have documentation regarding who to contact in an emergency. A homeless person could be familiar to the local police or director of a homeless shelter. Use of the internet has been effective in identifying family members of someone once viewed as an unrepresented patient.

- Regularly reassess rather than assume a patient's incapacitated state is permanent. Patients move in and out of decision-making capacity due to illness, medication and various therapeutic interventions.

- Conduct, when feasible, a formal psychiatric consult that is ordered by the attending physician. Ambiguity about whether a patient has mental capacity should not be resolved by a subjective evaluation by well-intentioned but unqualified staff members.

- Address patients' preferences prior to them becoming incapacitated. This is not a pleasant consideration, but psychiatric advance directives are authorized in 27 states, and there is a growing movement to have conventional advance directives supplemented with an advance directive for dementia. Nonetheless, the benefits associated with taking steps to maximize clarity and control should not be denied to current or prospective patients.

- Provide both staff and community education programs to help clinicians and local citizens understand the complexities associated with incapacitated, unrepresented patients. Such programs will demonstrate that the hospital recognizes its ethical obligation to meet the legitimate and continuing needs of this growing number of people who cannot make their own decisions and may lack suitable advocates.

- Host a lunch meeting with court-appointed conservators who are generally not enthusiastic about using their authority to give consent authorizations on behalf of unrepresented patients who lack decision-making capacity. The more hospitals and local conservators know about their respective constraints and issues affecting the entire process, the greater the likelihood of mutual understanding and perhaps more rapid decision making.

CONCLUDING OBSERVATIONS

Incapacitated, unrepresented patients are in a very precarious position. Helping such patients is usually time-consuming and the investment is often underappreciated, but early and tenacious attempts can be very productive and permit hospitals to serve all patients more effectively.

Our peripatetic population seems to be more disconnected. Many people across the country are struggling financially, physically and emotionally. Hospitals witness the impact of these struggles on a regular basis. Incapacitated, unrepresented patients are clearly among the most vulnerable members of our society. We can and should do better.

Originally published in the May/June 2019 issue of *Healthcare Executive* magazine.

Discussion Questions

Of the nine recommendations in the column, select four you believe will be the most effective and provide your rationale.

In addition to the author's suggestions, what other steps might be taken to identify a decision maker for an incapacitated or unrepresented patient?

Are Your Hospitalists Trained on the Issues?

Paul B. Hofmann, DrPH, LFACHE

THE NUMBER OF HOSPITALISTS in the United States has grown to more than 60,000 from just a few hundred, when the term was coined in 1996. Seventy-five percent of hospital patients are now treated by hospitalists, making it one of the fastest growing specialties in medicine, according to a 2018 report by the Society of Hospital Medicine. Given the increased number of hospitalists treating patients, what steps should be taken to enable hospitalists to become more effective at dealing with ethical dilemmas, particularly when most of them have not had a long-term patient relationship in contrast with primary care physicians and specialists who usually get to know their patients during office visits?

THE CASE FOR MORE ETHICS GUIDANCE

The July 1, 2019, issue of *Medical Ethics Advisor* included an insightful summary of a study performed at NewYork-Presbyterian Hospital/ Weill Cornell Medical Center, New York City. The study was initiated because a hospitalist was surprised to learn how many ethical issues were raised during daily rounds. Some surrogate decision makers appeared to be making poor decisions on patients' behalf. In addition, ethical issues of futility and allocation of resources were not being fully explored.

For the study, data was collected on 270 patients from September 2017 through May 2018. Among these patients, 77 had a total of 113 ethical issues relevant to their care. However, only five formal consults were brought to the facility's ethics committee. The concerns involved treatment refusals, goals of care, decision-making capacity and issues pertaining to medical futility. Although not every ethical question requires an ethics consult, the study's authors indicated it was "unclear whether the hospitalists knew there was an ethical issue and determined a consult was not necessary or whether the ethical issue simply went unrecognized."

As mentioned previously, complicating the entire process related to hospitalists and ethics is the absence of a relationship with patients similar to that between an office physician and a patient who normally selects that provider and sees him or her somewhat frequently. For hospitalists, "You are literally meeting a stranger at the bedside, and that person has to develop a relationship that is meaningful, and do so quickly during the stress of hospitalization," one of the study's authors stated.

Compounding the difficulty further is the stress many hospitalists experience. Rahulkumar Singh, MD, a hospitalist, wrote in a March 28, 2019, blog post for KevinMD.com that the hospitalist position "has been inherently more prone to burnout and is turning out to be a major challenge for leadership to deal with irrespective of the size or location of the program. While discussing this with our colleagues," he stated, "one statement which stuck with me is, 'Hospitalist programs are burnout factories.'" It's clear that giving more attention to building resiliency and reducing burnout among staff who are dealing more frequently with moral and emotional distress is paramount.

RECOMMENDATIONS

Given the need to focus more attention to the ethical issues confronted by hospitalists and the pressures many are encountering, what should hospital executives do to ameliorate the conditions described above? The following steps should be considered:

Survey the organization's hospitalists to evaluate their familiarity with ethical issues and available resources. Questions to consider include: Did you know the organization has an internal ethics committee? Do you know how to refer a case to the ethics committee? A survey should also ask what respondents believe the top three roles of the ethics committee should be and the expected outcomes or results they would like to receive from an ethics consultation.

Convene a focus group to engage hospitalists in an exploration of typical ethical dilemmas. This conversation will probably confirm a recognition of similar issues.

Encourage hospitalists to facilitate family conferences with other caregivers and patient relatives to help reconcile different perspectives. Involve a patient's closest friend or a member of the clergy when the patient has no known family members. Whenever possible, include patients who have decision-making capacity in these conferences.

Invite hospitalists to participate periodically in ethics rounds conducted in the intensive care unit, ED, neonatal intensive care unit and other patient units.

Develop in-service educational programs designed specifically for hospitalists. For example, assist them in learning about the value of preventive ethics by anticipating potential issues and providing insights to mitigate problems.

Include at least one hospitalist on the ethics committee. By becoming familiar with the committee's educational, policy development, and revision and consulting roles, the hospitalist will acquire direct appreciation for the committee's contribution to improving patient care. In addition, other committee members will benefit by learning more about the ethical dilemmas faced by hospitalists.

For a variety of reasons, not all healthcare facilities have hospitalists or can provide professional ethics consultation services. Nonetheless, the rapid growth in the number of hospitalists and the value of having ethics consultation services are indisputable. Strengthening the ethical skills of today's hospitalists will clearly benefit them but, perhaps more importantly, will also benefit their institutions, patients and families.

Originally published in the March/April 2020 issue of *Healthcare Executive* magazine.

Discussion Questions

Considering hospitalists have been increasingly involved in providing patient care for more than 20 years, why do you think the need for ethical education has been recognized only recently?

How would you prioritize the six steps proposed by the author, and why?

Stress Among Healthcare Professionals Calls Out for Attention

Paul B. Hofmann, DrPH, LFACHE

IT IS NO EXAGGERATION to suggest that hospitals can be unintentional incubators of intolerable stress. Emergency physician Natalie Newman has noted that "it almost seems as if the medical industry is designed to destroy the very people who practice within it" (Newman, 2018). Compassion fatigue is a real phenomenon, and the need for physical fatigue management policies in hospitals is clear (Hofmann, 2009, 2015).

Burnout harms everyone involved—not just healthcare professionals but also their families, patients, and institutions. The creation of programs to build staff resiliency should be a priority for healthcare leaders who are serious about building and sustaining healthier settings for the delivery of care. They must devote special attention to reducing the stress and burnout that healthcare professionals experience. Otherwise, the costs can be extremely high.

Nurses are twice as likely to suffer depression as the general population (Hofmann & Reed, 2016), and the suicide rate for physicians is higher than that for any other profession (Genovese & Berkek, 2016), in part because of the stress of medical school, malpractice suits, bullying, hazing, and sleep deprivation (Wible, 2018). Considering that the Centers for Disease Control and Prevention has reported a 25 percent increase in suicides from 1999 to 2016 in the general population (Carey, 2018), the degree of persistent and intolerable adversity that healthcare workers struggle with is especially worrisome.

The Joint Commission (2018) has issued an advisory to hospitals urging greater consideration for the needs of "second victims"—staff members involved in an adverse patient event. According to research cited in the advisory, affected staff can experience difficulty sleeping, reduced job satisfaction, guilt and anxiety (including fear of litigation or job loss), and recurrent memories of the event, all of which can contribute to more serious consequences such as burnout, depression, post-traumatic stress disorder, and suicidal ideation.

A 2017 study of patient safety officers at all of Maryland's acute care hospitals highlighted barriers that kept staff from obtaining help after an adverse event. "Chief among these barriers," the study reported, "was fear about confidentiality, negative judgment by coworkers, and the stigma of using such services" (Headley, 2018). Meanwhile, the annual costs of burnout-related turnover may be as high as $17 billion for all U.S. doctors and an additional $9 billion for nurses (National Taskforce on Humanity in Healthcare, 2018).

Given the growing awareness and high cost of this anxiety, why is the response still insufficient in healthcare? Three reasons are apparent to me:

1. The number of caregivers at risk in an increasingly frenetic work environment is growing, and leaders are unsure how to deal with the issue.
2. The continued impact of unrelenting stress on healthcare professionals has such a large and lasting ripple effect that many leaders believe the problem defies objective measurement and productive solutions.
3. Well-intentioned programs for addressing stress can provide a false sense of accomplishment when their actual impact is minimal because of poor design or execution.

KEY PLANNING STRATEGIES FOR SENIOR EXECUTIVES

A genuinely effective stress reduction program requires careful planning. A logic model approach can be effective and should start by defining succinct goals to impose discipline on the plan, such as an increase in staff satisfaction and a reduction in staff turnover and vacancy rates. With defined goals in place, the following components should be included (W.K. Kellogg Foundation, 2006):

- *Rationale* explains the need for the program.
- *Assumptions* are the beliefs about why the program will work.
- *Inputs* are the resources (human, financial, organizational, and community) that must be present for the program to succeed.
- *Activities* are the planned tasks for program implementation.
- *Outputs* are the services and products the program provides, including the target dates of service delivery; they should be SMART (specific, measurable, action oriented, realistic, and time bound).
- *Outcomes* are specific changes in attitudes, knowledge, behaviors, or health status expected to result from program activities and outputs; outcomes should also be SMART.
- *Impacts* are the long-term social or system changes the program aims to create.

However, applying the logic model process alone cannot reduce caregiver stress. In addition to unambiguous metrics and performance indicators with reliable baseline measures (as reflected in physician and employee satisfaction surveys), other strategies should be applied. For example, staff affected by burnout should be engaged in the planning process, proven interventions should be reinforced with sufficient resources, and evidence-based best management practices for combating burnout that have been successful in other organizations should be replicated and monitored.

EXAMPLES OF INNOVATIVE PROGRAMS

Ronald A. Paulus, MD, president and CEO of Mission Health in Asheville, North Carolina, and healthcare consultant David R. Strand based their burnout reduction strategy on three initiatives (Paulus and Strand, 2017):

1. Removing hassles and scaling joys in the practice environment
2. Increasing team communication with an emphasis on strengths, values, and goals
3. Enhancing individual resiliency and well-being by equipping clinicians to manage stress using evidence-based skills

Paulus and Strand (2017) recommend targeting a "well-being ROI [return on investment]" that includes both financial returns and patient impact. The right kind of leadership, they contend, can change the trajectory and restore joy and humanity to healthcare delivery.

Tom Jenike, MD, chief human experience officer at Novant Health in Winston-Salem, North Carolina, promotes the Novant Health Leadership Development Program, which involves an intensive three-day workshop and then ongoing connection with "graduates." Since 2013, approximately 800 physicians have completed the training curriculum developed by Jenike and a professional coach. In addition, about 900 nurses have completed a version of the course tailored to nurses.

By 2016, the Novant program's ROI became demonstrably clear. Physicians who completed the program scored in the 97th percentile for satisfaction on the Press Ganey survey, whereas Novant's non-participants scored in the 50th percentile. The rate of physician turnover fell, and open positions in the medical group were filled more quickly and easily. Reflecting a shift in organizational culture, the challenges of healthcare are now openly discussed, and clinicians step forward when they are concerned about colleagues. Participants have described the program as "life changing" in their feedback. In addition, leadership has received letters from spouses of participants thanking them for the changes they see in their loved ones (Shannon, 2018).

Not surprisingly, the Mayo Clinic is taking a leadership role in this challenging area. Colin West, MD, codirector of Mayo's Department of Medicine Physician Well-Being Program, and his colleagues have published more than a hundred papers on physician burnout. In 2017, the clinic's president and CEO, John Noseworthy, MD, and 10 other prominent health system CEOs authored a *Health Affairs* article that characterized physician burnout as a public health crisis and called for action by senior management (Noseworthy et al., 2017).

CONCLUSION

The cliché that culture eats strategy for lunch is especially relevant in a discussion of improving the working environment in healthcare. An organizational culture of individual infallibility that demands perfection in job performance is inappropriate and counterproductive to efforts to improve care. Conversely, "if burnout is effectively and respectfully addressed, health care organizations can create environments that help physicians and other providers achieve a healthy work–life balance while providing the highest quality care to their patients" (Jenike, 2016).

A goal of zero harm to patients is a laudable and reasonable objective; it motivates staff to follow proper policies and procedures, report near misses, perform root-cause analyses, and reduce preventable errors. Although a goal of zero harm to staff may be more problematic to achieve, the need to make our institutions less toxic for caregivers is an irrefutable, ethical imperative.

REFERENCES

Carey, B. (2018, June 7). Defying prevention efforts, suicide rates are climbing across the country. *New York Times*. Retrieved from www.nytimes.com/2018/06/07/health/suicide-rates-kate-spade.html

Genovese, J., & Berkek, J. (2016). Can arts and communication programs improve physician wellness and mitigate physician suicide? *Journal of Clinical Oncology, 34*(15), 1820–1822.

Headley, M. (2018). Are second victims getting the help they need? *Patient Safety & Quality Healthcare, 15*(2), 12–16.

Hofmann, P. (2009). Addressing compassion fatigue. *Healthcare Executive, 24*(5), 40–42.

Hofmann, P. (2015). The urgent need for fatigue management policies. *Healthcare Executive, 30*(5), 48, 50–51.

Hofmann, P., & Reed, J. (2016, May 9). Why suicide prevention is part of population health strategy. *Hospitals and Health Networks Daily*. Retrieved from www.hhnmag.com/articles/7174-why-suicideprevention-is-part-of-population-health-strategy

Jenike, T. (2016, June 29). Fighting the silent crisis of physician burnout. STAT. Retrieved from https://www.statnews.com/2016/06/29/fighting-physician-burnout

Joint Commission. (2018, January 22). Supporting second victims. *Quick Safety*. Retrieved from www.jointcommission.org/assets/1/23/Quick_Safety_Issue_39_2017_Second_victim_FINAL2.pdf

National Taskforce on Humanity in Healthcare. (2018, April 25). *The business case for humanity in healthcare* [Position paper]. Retrieved from http://blog.mission-health.org/wp-content/uploads/sites/2/2018/04/NTH-Business-Case_final.pdf

Newman, N. (2018, April 2). What this doctor decided to do about physician suicide [Web log post]. Retrieved from www.kevinmd.com/blog/2018/03/doctor-decided-physician-suicide.html

Noseworthy, J., Madara, J., Cosgrove, D., Edgeworth, M., Ellison, E., Krevans, S., . . . & Harrison, D. (2017, March 18). Physician burnout is a public health crisis: A message to our fellow health care CEOs [*Health Affairs* Web log post]. Retrieved from www.healthleadersmedia.com/strategy/physician-burnout-public-health-crisis-message-our-fellow-healthcare-ceos

Paulus, R., & Strand, D. (2017). Dousing clinician burnout. *Trustee, 70*(7), 26–27.

Shannon, D. (2018, January 18). Physician burnout is caused by systems problems. Here's how to fix that [KevinMD.com Web log post]. Retrieved from www.kevinmd.com/blog/2018/01/physician-burnout-caused-systems-problems-heres-fix.html

Wible, P. (2018, January 13). What I've learned from my tally of 757 doctor suicides. *Washington Post.* Retrieved from www.washingtonpost.com/national/health-science/what-ive-learned-from-my-tally-of-757-doctor-suicides/2018/01/12/b0ea9126-eb50-11e7-9f92-10a2203f6c8d_story.html

W.K. Kellogg Foundation. (2006). *W.K. Kellogg Foundation logic model development guide.* Retrieved from www.wkkf.org/resource-directory/resource/2006/02/wk-kellogg-foundation-logic-model-development-guide

Originally published in the September/October 2018 issue of the *Journal of Healthcare Management*.

Discussion Questions

Of the three reasons for an insufficient response to reducing stress, which one do you believe is most responsible, and why?

The COVID-19 pandemic has heightened the level of burnout experienced by all hospital staff members. What more can hospitals do to mitigate this problem?

Empathy's Role in Improving Resiliency

Paul B. Hofmann, DrPH, LFACHE

GIVEN THE UNPRECEDENTED IMPACT of the coronavirus pandemic, accelerating steps needed to elevate empathetic behavior is especially important. A psychologically safe and just culture will assist staff and patients in coping more effectively when uncertainty and fear are so ubiquitous. There is no panacea, but each incremental effort will be worth the investment.

In her notable 2013 TED Talk, Harvard professor and psychiatrist Helen Riess, MD, provides several breathtaking examples of human empathy (see sidebar below). During the talk Riess says, "The good news about empathy is that when it declines, it can also be learned. Employers who want to have an engaged and productive workforce need to get tuned into the people. Patients who don't feel cared about have longer recovery rates and poor immune function."

During an extended phone conversation I had with Riess early this year, she emphasized that the qualities of empathy are teachable and, eventually, lead to an improvement in staff attitudes and behavior.

More recently, she told me, "During the COVID-19 pandemic, empathy is needed more than ever at every level of healthcare organizations. Our patients need greater empathy because of the increased threats to their safety, and our colleagues need support and permission to ask for help that may be difficult for them."

Riess created the acronym E-M-P-AT-H-Y to help us remember the key pieces of how we connect to people. In the TED Talk, she describes:

- The "E" represents eye contact. Every human being, Riess says, "has a longing to be seen, understood and appreciated."
- The "M" represents facial expression muscles. Riess suggests our faces are actually a road map of human emotion that can rarely be completely hidden.
- The "P" represents posture. Riess indicates "posture is another powerful conveyor of connection." She cites a widely publicized study (*Journal of Pain and Symptom Management*, May 2005) in which researchers at MD Anderson Cancer Center in Houston found that physicians who were asked to sit down when making rounds in a patient's room were rated as being much warmer and more caring and were estimated to have spent three to five times longer with their patients than doctors who remained standing, even though both sets of physicians spent the same amount of time with patients.
- The "A" represents affect. Physicians are trained to evaluate a patient's affect as a way of assessing the person's emotional state.
- The "T" represents tone of voice. According to Riess, the nuclei for tone of voice and facial expression reside in the same area of our brain stems. "This means that when we are emotionally activated, our tone of voice and our facial expressions change without our even trying," Riess says. With practice, Riess notes, we can become more capable of hearing and seeing what these emotions are.
- The "H" represents hearing the whole person. "Far more than the words that people say, hearing the whole person

means understanding the context in which other people live," Riess says.

- The "Y" represents one's response to others' feelings. "We respond to other people's feelings all the time," Riess says. "We might think that we only experience our own emotions, but we're constantly absorbing the feelings of others."

The Power of Empathy

Harvard professor and psychiatrist Helen Riess, MD, works at Massachusetts General Hospital and is the co-founder, chief scientist and chair of Empathetics Inc. Her remarkable 2013 TED Talk, "The Power of Empathy," has been viewed over 500,000 times.

During the talk, Riess mentions having received a request from one of her students who wanted to determine if, when there is empathy between people, their heart rates and other physiological tracers become concordant. The student also wanted to recruit doctor–patient pairs who were willing to have their sessions videotaped and be hooked up to monitoring devices during those sessions. Riess approved the project, participated in it and, in the TED Talk, explains how she became a more effective therapist as a result of analyzing the videos. According to Riess, the familiar statement, "I feel your pain," is actually validated by neuron studies of the brain.

This experience led her to learn everything she could about the neuroscience of empathy which, in turn, motivated her to develop empathy training grounded in the neurobiology of emotions and empathy. The training was evaluated in a randomized control trial where those doctors trained in empathy were reported by patients as being better listeners, showing more compassion and better understanding patient concerns.

THE IMPORTANCE OF UNHURRIED CONVERSATIONS

The article "Careful and Kind Care Requires Unhurried Conversations," published in the October 29, 2019, issue of *NEJM Catalyst*, highlights a similar theme. According to the authors, "To enable unhurried conversations, whether face-to-face, via telemedicine, asynchronous or virtual, participants need to make themselves cognitively and emotionally available."

It is true that the term "unhurried conversations" implies that such discussions will take more time than perhaps is desired when there are intense pressures on clinicians to increase productivity, see more patients and become more efficient. However, reality and perception are not always aligned. This familiar adage was confirmed by five noteworthy articles: the previously cited 2005 issue of the *Journal of Pain and Symptom Management*; a 2011 issue of *Patient Education and Counseling*; a 2016 issue of the *Patient Experience Journal*; a 2016 issue of the *Journal of Hospital Medicine*; and a 2017 issue of the *Journal of Nursing Care Quality*. Each article reported the results of studies that consistently demonstrated that patients perceived doctors and nurses spending more time with them than other clinicians when the staff member simply sat down.

In an article I co-authored with Jeffrey Selberg in the January/February 2006 issue of *Healthcare Executive*, we recommended several steps that should be taken to promote a culture of empathy. At least three deserve re-emphasis:

- Establish objective performance indicators, standards and goals regarding patient-centered care; monitor results; and routinely report findings to senior management, medical staff leadership and board members.
- Create opportunities for patients and family members to promote quality healthcare and improve workflow processes by serving on hospital advisory committees.

- Insist that senior executives make regular patient rounds to remind them of the value of interacting directly with patients and staff on clinical units.

Given our experience with COVID-19, we know resources and time are going to be insufficient to meet the needs of every clinician. Consequently, any program that promotes empathy and benefits patients as well as staff by increasing their resiliency in the face of pandemics, illness, trauma or occupational stress should be pursued vigorously.

Originally published in the July/August 2020 issue of *Healthcare Executive* magazine.

Discussion Questions

Given persuasive evidence that physicians and nurses who sit down rather than stand are consistently perceived by patients as being more empathetic, what can hospitals do to encourage this behavior?

How can reservations about appointing patients and family members to hospital advisory committees to promote quality healthcare and improve workflow processes be best addressed?

Ethics Consults Versus Legal Advice

Paul B. Hofmann, DrPH, LFACHE

ETHICAL AND LEGAL DILEMMAS are invariably complex and daunting. Their resolution requires sensitivity and careful deliberation to ensure appropriate outcomes.

ETHICS CONSULTATIONS

Traditionally, ethics consults are requested in cases where ethical dilemmas have not been resolved on clinical units. Such cases typically involve disagreements among family members of a patient lacking decision-making capacity and an advance directive.

In other situations, a patient without an advance directive and who is lacking decision-making capacity may be unrepresented, with no relative or close friend who can speak on behalf of the patient's values and best interests.

Cases that lack easy resolution become even more challenging in the absence of consensus among treating physicians or if a court-appointed conservator takes a position contrary to the outcome of an ethics consult.

Complicating these circumstances further, nurses and other caregivers frequently experience moral distress in situations where patients have a low likelihood of survival. In these situations, continuing invasive treatment is viewed as nonbeneficial and even harmful.

In addition to legitimate concerns regarding staff morale, other patients needing admission to the ICU may not have timely access, and high financial costs are incurred.

Most members of the community are unaware of the innumerable hours hospital and health system ethics committees devote to individual cases, always with the goal of reaching a recommendation reflecting not only the patient's best interest but also the institution's values.

Ethics Committees: A Brief History

When the American Hospital Association's Special Committee on Bioethics issued its 1985 guidelines on the role of hospital ethics committees, we emphasized that ethics consults were recommendations for consideration by a patient's attending physician. They were advisory only with the ultimate decision left to the physician. At that time, the Joint Commission on Accreditation of Healthcare Organizations (now The Joint Commission) asked if a JCAHO Standard should be adopted to require all hospitals to have an ethics committee. As the special committee's chairman at the time, I said every hospital should have a process that allows staff, patients and families to address ethical issues, but while an ethics committee would be helpful, it should not be mandatory. In 1992, JCAHO established a requirement that healthcare institutions "have in place a mechanism for the consideration of ethical issues arising in the care of patients."

LEGAL CONSULTATIONS

In addition to ethical considerations, another key party becomes involved in some cases—the hospital's legal counsel. Most hospitals do not have a full-time, in-house attorney, especially smaller hospitals. Instead, they rely on an outside law firm.

Depending on the size of the firm and other variables, the attorney may not be engaged exclusively or even primarily with healthcare issues. He or she acts in an advisory capacity similar to whomever is providing an ethics consult.

But there is a fundamental difference in the focus of legal counsel. In contrast to the conventional ethics consult, which gives priority to the patient's best interest and the institution's values, most attorneys concentrate on resolutions that prevent or minimize potential liability exposure. Ideally, these objectives will be aligned, but this is not consistently true.

For example, in one case the hospital's outside attorney advised against complying with an ethics consult recommendation that a patient's advance directive be followed. This advice was provided even though the patient handwrote a phrase making clear her wishes to receive comfort measures only and not to be transferred to a skilled nursing facility.

The attorney was concerned a family member might possibly sue the hospital, and senior management accepted the attorney's advice.

As another example, a patient may have signed a legally valid "Provider Orders for Life-Sustaining Treatment" form to improve end-of-life care, which encourages providers to speak with patients and create specific medical orders to be honored by healthcare workers during a medical crisis.

Yet, we know nursing home patients and others with POLST forms are sometimes inappropriately taken to hospital EDs when they are dying.

Emergency department physicians may not see the form and will feel compelled to institute aggressive treatment.

Furthermore, we have found that conservators can be unfamiliar with POLST forms and not appreciate why their content is so crucial to honoring a patient's preferences.

RECOMMENDATIONS FOR LEADERS

Fundamental to reducing tension and a divergence between support-ing patients and respecting the role of attorneys and conservators is mutual education.

Those performing ethics consults and other stakeholders com-mitted to minimizing liability exposure or safeguarding the rights of unrepresented patients are urged to develop a sound understanding of their respective responsibilities.

Healthcare leaders are encouraged to consider the following steps:

- When feasible, have the hospital's attorney and risk manager attend regular ethics committee meetings. Some committees also have the benefit of a community member who is a lawyer.

- Hospitals without an in-house counsel or that are part of a health system that does not have a full-time attorney can consider making a special effort to orient the attorney who provides assistance to the board on legal matters. This person could be the most likely contact when an ethics consult has possible liability implications.

- Host a lunch meeting with conservators and ethics committee members. This approach is so participants can acquire a deeper appreciation of the often-formidable challenges associated with their functions.

- Partner with a local medical society and bar association in promoting an educational seminar to discuss how tough ethical cases were resolved through a collaborative process.

- Create a hospital policy and procedure concerning medical decision-making for the incapacitated, unrepresented patient with the input and support of the ethics committee and the hospital's attorney. (See the Healthcare Management Ethics column on this topic in the May/June 2019 issue of *Healthcare Executive*.)

Any initiative that achieves greater harmony among ethics committees, hospital attorneys and conservators is worth the effort.

Originally published in the November/December 2020 issue of *Healthcare Executive* magazine.

Discussion Questions

If you were the chair or a member of an ethics committee that had reached a conscientious recommendation that was overruled by both the hospital's legal counsel and senior management, what would you do?

If nursing home patients with POLST forms are inappropriately being taken to hospital ERs when they are dying so the nursing home can avoid issues related to patient deaths, how might this concern be addressed?

Conflicts of Interest

William A. Nelson, PhD, HFACHE

CONFLICTS OF INTEREST ARE an increasing concern across almost every sector, including business, government, politics, finance, education, and healthcare. Newspapers are filled with stories of the fallout stemming from institutions and people involved in conflict of interest situations. Healthcare certainly is not immune to these concerns.

According to a 2005 survey of physician executives published in *Physician Executive*, 90 percent of the respondents were very concerned or moderately concerned about unethical business practices. Sixty-six percent of the respondents further indicated they were concerned about nonphysician executives' and board members' conflicts of interest. As a result, healthcare facilities need to develop approaches for recognizing, managing, and preventing conflicts of interest.

DEFINING CONFLICTS OF INTEREST

Managing conflicts of interest requires a clear understanding of what the concept entails. A suggested definition is: Conflicts of interest occur when self-interest affects an individual's professional obligations to one's patients, organization, and/or profession. A similar definition states: Conflicts of interest occur when a personal or private interest influences (or appears to influence) a professional's objective judgment and the exercise of that individual's recognized duty.

Even lacking a uniform definition, the various definitions reflect the basic components for a conflict of interest to occur:

- **Self-interest and/or personal interest:** The self-interest often is described as financial, but it also can include providing a special advantage to a friend, business associate, relative, vendor, or supplier.

- **Professional and/or organization duty:** Healthcare executives are expected to be competent and fulfill their responsibilities in a manner that reflects their profession's standards, including its code of ethics. Additionally, executives and other healthcare organization staff have an obligation to direct their activities and decisions to fulfill the mission and values of their organization.

The conflict of interest occurs when one's self-interest or personal interest interferes with or alters objective professional judgments or actions. Healthcare professionals are respected not only because of their recognized competence, but also because they carry a public expectation that they will act on behalf of and in the best interest of patients and the organization's mission. Therefore, conflicts of interest undermine the fundamental fiduciary obligation of a professional and a healthcare organization to provide quality patient care.

Because everyone has a certain level of self-interest, such as wanting to receive an appropriate salary for a position, it can be unclear in certain situations whether a person's self-interest has crossed the threshold and is in fact a conflict of interest. Some have suggested a form of trust assessment because at the heart of conflicts of interest is a betrayal of trust. Ask yourself this question: Would your patients, employer, professional colleagues, the board, and the public trust your judgment regarding a particular decision or action if they knew you had a personal interest in it?

Ethical concerns also are raised when an individual's conflict of interest can, and most likely will, negatively impact the organization's integrity and commitment to its mission and value statements. In a very real and practical way, any conflict of interest will also lessen the community's image of the involved individual(s) and the organization.

PREVENTING CONFLICTS OF INTEREST

Directed by executive leaders, organizations should develop and pursue approaches to manage and prevent the occurrence of these detrimental situations. Several basic strategies have been suggested for preventing conflicts in today's healthcare setting. The article "Practicing Preventive Ethics—The Keys to Avoiding Ethical Conflicts in Health Care" by L. McCullough, published in *Physician Executive* (March/April 2005, 31(2):18–21), suggests the following:

- Continually emphasize and foster the fiduciary commitment of professionalism throughout the organization's culture and practices.
- Mission statements and policies should reflect an explicit commitment to the fiduciary responsibility of professionals and the organization to promote quality of care.
- Develop, implement and enforce a conflict of interest policy. The policy should be appropriately detailed, beginning with a statement of purpose and definition of the concept. The policy should include examples of conflicts of interest; require that all business, supplier, and vendor relationships be self-reported, including any gift and/or payment; describe the review process for assessing potential conflicts of interest; describe a method for others (whistleblowers) to report a potential conflict; provide provisions for the enforcement of violations; and indicate the resources for clarifying the policy when needed.

Two additional components to a policy relate to managing potential conflicts. First, the policy should designate an office or person to guide clinicians or healthcare executives prior to accepting a relationship or activity with a healthcare supplier. Second, because disclosure of potential conflicts is essential, the review process should clarify whether the disclosed situation creates a conflict of interest for the individual or the organization.

Clearly not all relationships between administrators or clinicians and associations, businesses, or vendors create a conflict of interest. In some situations such relationships are beneficial. However, to avoid public misperception, the organization, after reviewing such situations through the conflict-of-interest policy review process, should publicly disclose all appropriate relationships with vendors, suppliers, and other business relationships, including payments received. One major medical center is developing a public website that will list all its staff's consulting arrangements, including the payments received. Such a high level of transparency, similar to the sharing of quality and outcome reports and the costs of healthcare treatments, fosters trust in the organization.

When drafting or updating a conflict of interest policy as suggested above, the ACHE ethical policy statement "Considerations for Healthcare Executive–Supplier Interactions," available on **ache. org**, should be used as a model resource.

Conflicts of interest are a serious concern that undermines the integrity of professionals and an organization's fiduciary responsibility to its patients and the community. An aggressive program that recognizes, manages and seeks to prevent conflicts of interest is essential despite the many complications that surround the concept of conflicts of interest. As with other organizational policies, an effective program to manage conflicts of interest can be achieved only through leadership that demonstrates the importance of avoiding conflicts of interest and supports a comprehensive educational effort propagating the policy and rigorous adherence to its implementation.

Originally published in the March/April 2009 issue of *Healthcare Executive* magazine.

Discussion Questions

Conflicts of interest are a common phenomenon in health-care organizations. Identify several examples of how conflicts of interest can undermine patient care.

If you were drafting guidelines for clinicians to prevent conflicts of interests, what would be some of the key features?

Recruiting Retired Clinicians

Paul B. Hofmann, DrPH, LFACHE,
and Douglas Van Houten, RN

WITH RAPID SURGES IN the number of COVID-19 patients happening throughout the crisis, the need for swift deployment of additional doctors, nurses and other clinicians to support exhausted healthcare professionals has been obvious.

In normal times, hospitals routinely turn to registries and contract workers for nursing assistance, and nurse staffing agencies typically are accountable for handling payroll and confirming maintenance of required qualifications, licenses and certifications. Under present circumstances, however, these resources are limited. As a result, organizations are reaching out to retired nurses, physicians and others directly to relieve some of the intense pressure and burnout affecting their current staff members. Such an effort is reasonable and laudable, but it should be undertaken carefully and systematically.

Some of the questions organizational leadership should consider when recruiting retired clinicians include:

- What institutional orientation programs are needed for clinicians who have retired from other facilities to familiarize them with the organization's culture, management structure, programs and policies?
- How can the current qualifications, skill sets and cognitive abilities of all individuals be accurately assessed?

- What steps should be taken to evaluate the clinician's physical and emotional capacity to cope with workload demands in advance of his or her appointment or employment?

- Should special arrangements be made to monitor the recruited clinicians' performance and, if so, by whom?

- Is there value in convening periodic meetings of this unique cohort of individuals to encourage sharing of experiences and insights? Who might facilitate the meetings and plan the agenda?

- Would it be useful to appoint a small multidisciplinary task force to oversee the reentry program and determine if some returning clinicians would benefit from having a designated mentor?

- How often should surveys be distributed to formerly retired clinicians who have reentered the workforce, and what issues should be covered?

- What additional steps can be taken to prevent and mitigate compassion fatigue and moral distress as surging admissions overburden the team?

The last question's importance is reflected in a very poignant commentary authored by palliative care physician Richard E. Leiter, MD, of Dana-Farber/Brigham and Women's Hospital, Boston. Writing in the December 31, 2020, issue of the *New England Journal of Medicine,* he says, "Inundated with reports of new waves of COVID battering our colleagues around the United States, I worry that we're all at increased risk for anxiety, depression, and post-traumatic stress disorder. . . . While we try to heal from the collective trauma we experienced in our hospital over the worst four months of the local epidemic, I struggle to know where to look. Peering into the future, given what we see on the news, saturates me with dread. And yet it's too early to look back. Perspective can't develop in the presence of open wounds." The call for relief for clinician stress and burnout is clear.

RECOMMENDATIONS FOR HEALTHCARE LEADERS

Recommendations for healthcare leaders to consider when recruiting and integrating retired clinicians into their workforces include:

- Learn from other organizations about their cumulative experience in implementing successful reentry programs for health professionals; ask for information concerning initial problems encountered and how they overcame them.
- Determine if the approaches to recruiting retired physicians, nurses, respiratory therapists and other clinicians varied, obtaining the rationale for these differences.
- Maximize the utilization of trusted contract services to reduce time and administrative barriers to engaging reentry clinical professionals.
- Ask about the most productive methods for reaching the maximum number of potentially qualified candidates to reenter their profession, such as advertising, hosting a virtual or in-person welcome-back event, and engaging local and state professional societies.
- Explore whether the organizations addressed the questions posed at the beginning of this column and how they were answered.
- Consider developing an incentive program to motivate current clinicians who are personally responsible for successfully recruiting a former colleague.
- Encourage professional societies to coordinate presentations featuring speakers who would describe their experience in launching and maintaining effective reentry programs.

Recruiting the right retired clinician and placing her or him in a position that will benefit colleagues and patients is not a simple process. It is worth undertaking now, however, and will help put a reliable system in place when it is needed in the future.

Other Timely Articles

In **January 2020, the** *Journal of the American Medical Association* published articles on Yale New Haven Hospital's policy requiring cognitive testing in the recredentialing process for physicians 70 and older. Among Yale's older physicians, 12.6 percent demonstrated significant deficits.

A similar finding was reported in the **February 2021 issue of the** *NEJM Catalyst*. Hartford HealthCare instituted a program of provider assessment and cognitive screening of all clinicians at the age of 70. A 14.4 percent incidence of cognitive impairment was observed.

Writing in the **December 14, 2020, issue of the** *Hastings Center Report*, physician Tia Powell, MD, notes, ". . . roughly a quarter of practicing physicians are reportedly over sixty-five. We all face age-related changes in processing speed, memory, and executive function." She also indicates, "This is a classic public health ethics problem. How do we balance the rights and preferences of one group, aging doctors, against the public's right to receive safe and competent medical care?"

Finally, Powell notes, "Many institutions rely on peer review to recredential physicians, but this approach is ineffective alone, for assessments are too easily bent by subjective factors. . . . A just system would include objective measurements with national standards for appropriate cognitive testing; every institution should not create its own system. The designers of the tests should make them easy to administer and resistant to cheating, perhaps by creating a database of different versions randomly assigned."

Originally published in the May/June 2021 issue of *Healthcare Executive* magazine.

Discussion Questions

Assuming you agree with the importance of evaluating a retired clinician's physical and emotional capacity to cope with workload demands in advance of his or her appointment or employment, what process might be developed to best achieve this purpose?

What do you think are the most challenging issues associated with recruiting and retaining qualified retired clinicians, and how can those issues be minimized?

Accountability for Nosocomial Infections

Paul B. Hofmann, DrPH, LFACHE

THE DEVELOPMENT OF A nosocomial (hospital-acquired) infection is a classic example of an iatrogenic incident in hospitals and
nursing homes. Within my organization, I suspect some patients
are not informed that the infection is unrelated to their admitting
condition, unless they are already debilitated, and are unaware of
the additional length of stay it causes. What are the ethical, legal,
and financial issues that this topic raises, and how should they be
addressed?

This complex problem has only recently begun receiving the
attention it deserves. More than five years have passed since the
Institute of Medicine reported that up to 98,000 patients die each
year in hospitals due to clinical errors. Yet this large number did not
include all of the estimated 88,000 deaths that occur as the result
of nosocomial infections, which affect approximately two million
patients annually. Because a third of these infections are the direct
result of acts of commission and omission, they should be viewed
as clinical errors as well.

Ironically, some perverse financial benefits often accrue to the
organization when an infection happens. In more than 100 DRGs,
a hospital-acquired urinary tract infection causes the patient's care
to be classified as "complicated." Consequently, although hospital-
acquired infections are mostly preventable, reimbursement to the
hospital can almost double when they occur.

One of the most frequently omitted actions by caregivers is the simple act of hand washing. According to the CDC and the U.S. Department of Health and Human Services, strict adherence to hand-washing procedures alone could prevent the deaths of 20,000 patients each year. When the implementation of basic, inexpensive measures can have such an enormous impact, there is no excuse for not taking immediate action. We have the ability to prevent many infections from occurring and others from spreading, for example, methicillin-resistant *S. aureus* infections. Failing to do so is ethically indefensible. What inhibits hospitals and caregivers from ensuring that everyone is more vigilant?

ORGANIZATIONAL BARRIERS

Historically, a variety of organizational barriers, as well as human nature, have impeded more rapid progress in reducing nosocomial infections. These include:

- **Denial and rationalization.** It is relatively easy to avoid taking strong action when the problem either is not acknowledged or is viewed as one of the unavoidable risks of being hospitalized.
- **Failure to establish a culture of safety.** Unless organizations empower employees, physicians, and even patients and families to identify the risks of infections, important and indeed essential allies will have been ignored in dealing with this continuing challenge.
- **Culture of blame.** As opposed to a culture of safety where emphasis is placed on teamwork and preventing harm to patients, a culture of blame focuses on individuals and reprimands them for causing the harm. When this happens, out of fear of retribution, staff members are much less likely to acknowledge a mistake and suggest what can be done to avoid a recurrence.

- **Fear of liability.** Reticence to identify deficiencies is a classic component of a culture of blame, and this reticence is reinforced when there is a fear of punitive action in the form of legal action against the organization or the individual.

- **Inadequate education and training.** While everyone should be aware of the benefits of hand washing, providing repeated reminders about its importance helps achieve compliance. In addition, staff involved in the care of high-risk patients (for example, those in intensive care units) need to be carefully trained in the handling of intravenous lines and the changing of dressings to prevent infections. (For a case study in reducing catheter-related bloodstream infections, see page 20 of the March/April 2005 issue of *Healthcare Executive*.)

- **Resistance to change.** It is human nature for people to adopt habits or ways of performing their jobs that are convenient for them. These individuals are often unenthusiastic about modifying their behavior, particularly if they view the changes as interrupting their normal pattern of activity.

- **Deficient physical plant design.** Hand washing should be easy to do, especially now with alcohol-based hand rubs. However, sinks, alcohol-based hand rubs, and hand-washing solutions are often not close to the site of patient care and not readily convenient for use by caregivers.

- **Resource constraints.** Outmoded facilities, substandard staffing, and budget limitations make it more difficult to isolate infected and immunosuppressed patients, permit staff to follow and monitor proper infection control techniques, and purchase required equipment and supplies.

- **Lack of leadership and accountability.** Ultimately, the largest organizational barrier—as is usually the case with addressing any critical program—is the failure of administrative and clinical leaders to insist that this issue must be a high priority.

RESOLVING THE DILEMMA

A number of studies have now confirmed the obvious: Patients and their families recognize that even very competent staff members are fallible and make mistakes, but patients and their families do not understand, nor will they tolerate, cover-ups. Fortunately, they can be very effective allies in the patient care process. For example, asking staff members (physicians, nurses, or others) if they have washed their hands before conducting examinations, changing dressings, administering medication, and drawing blood can and does produce a marked improvement in hand-washing compliance.

Effective January of this year, the Joint Commission on Accreditation of Healthcare Organizations instituted new standards to cause facilities to focus more intensively on infection control procedures. All hospitals now must demonstrate compliance with handwashing practices established by the Centers for Disease Control and Prevention. Providers are also required to report as a sentinel event, and submit a plan of correction for, each identified case of unanticipated death or major, permanent loss of function associated with a nosocomial infection.

Acknowledging a mistake or problem has occurred, genuinely apologizing for it, describing precisely what measures have been taken to avoid or minimize recurrence if the probable cause is known, and—when suitable—offering some reasonable compensation are steps in a response that has two distinct advantages. First, it is the most ethically appropriate response, at least in part because this is the manner in which you or a member of your family would want to be treated in a similar situation. Second, unless legal counsel advises to the contrary, it is most likely to reduce the likelihood of a lawsuit and the financial costs associated with defending a potential malpractice case.

Any adverse event affecting a patient's treatment and/or length of stay is lamentable. Discussing the event in a timely and forthright manner with the patient is an ethical imperative that is also a legally and financially sound practice, and it should be included in every organization's policy on disclosing clinical mistakes. Now and in the future, we must continually ask ourselves why patients must suffer not just from injury or disease but also from their treatment. Only by having everyone focusing on preventing harm from occurring to patients will the incidence and sad consequences of preventable nosocomial infections be eliminated.

Originally published in the May/June 2005 issue of *Healthcare Executive* magazine.

Discussion Questions

Given that hospitals are sometimes reimbursed more when a patient's care is identified as "complicated," offer your views about how this issue can be properly addressed when many hospitals are struggling financially.

Nine possible organizational barriers to reducing hospital-acquired infections are listed. How would you rank them in importance, and why?

Addressing Compassion Fatigue

Paul B. Hofmann, DrPH, LFACHE

COMPASSION FATIGUE IS AN inability or reduced capacity to feel and convey genuine understanding, empathy and support. Few healthcare professionals are immune to compassion fatigue. It occurs most often when the need for compassion is great and seemingly unrelenting. In healthcare facilities, this problem usually exists when the level of stress is high, demand for attention is rising and emotional reserves appear insufficient to accommodate the needs of not only patients and families but also staff.

In the past, but presumably less so today, the very nature of medical education was blamed for dehumanizing altruistic, sensitive medical students and producing cold, impersonal and unsympathetic physicians. Some suggested it was essential the physician–patient relationship be kept as objective and formal as possible to maintain a professional rapport. Proponents of this approach said preserving a proper distance would protect physicians from becoming too vulnerable and emotionally involved with their patients.

There are, of course, other more prevalent factors leading to compassion fatigue among healthcare workers. They include lack of early encouragement from family to give and accept compassion; inadequate professional training; poor mentoring; low staffing; and an organizational culture that does not encourage, value and recognize exemplary displays of compassion.

Unquestionably, disruptive behavior of physicians, nurses, managers and others is another factor contributing to reduced compassion. Anyone who has been regularly berated and verbally abused will have a more difficult time compartmentalizing the resulting feelings and conveying compassion to patients, families and colleagues.

We know inconsiderate behavior by physicians and managers makes their subordinates' work more stressful. More specifically, if employees do not believe they are respected and appreciated for their efforts, and if they do not feel cared about by those who have responsibility for them, it will be more difficult for them to establish and sustain a truly caring environment for patients.

Also, in healthcare organizations that focus too narrowly on the achievement of standard measures, some staff members may concentrate exclusively on task completion as the goal rather than how the care is provided.

A colleague described a recent case where a Buddhist patient in the ICU suffered a prolonged and uncomfortable death. The patient's family had stood watch as the patient's condition deteriorated. After his death, when family members asked, based on cultural practices, if the body could lay undisturbed for a number of hours before being moved, the charge nurse denied the request.

The family members were told they had 15 minutes with their loved one because a patient in the emergency department needed the bed. In this situation, rather than working creatively to find another option that would meet the family's needs, the charge nurse focused only on the task at hand—prepare the ICU bed for the emergency department patient.

COSTS OF COMPASSION FATIGUE

In addition to patients and families, victims of compassion fatigue include clinical staff. Even nonclinical personnel, however, will be affected when workload exceeds capacity and personal and professional issues compromise normal coping techniques. Inevitably, compassion fatigue will have an adverse impact on staff recruitment, retention, morale and performance.

Predictably, those who are psychologically and physically exhausted will be less likely to show compassion. And unfortunately, in times of staff reductions and a struggling economy, the need for more compassion increases just when emotional reservoirs are lower.

According to a physician quoted in a February 6, 2009, *New York Times* article, doctors and nurses "feel trapped by the competing demands of administrators, insurance companies, lawyers, patients' families and even one another." There are no signs the intensity of these demands will diminish in the near future, so we must think creatively about how to confront them successfully.

ADDRESSING COMPASSION FATIGUE

Determine whether compassion fatigue is a valid concern within your organization, and involve your staff in preparing an action plan to eliminate it if possible or at least reduce it.

Recognize and celebrate uncommon displays of compassion to indicate that such behavior is genuinely appreciated and valued.

Consider job-sharing arrangements to allow personnel in particularly stressful positions to work in other settings as well. For example, in one health system, hospice social workers and nurses work one or two days a week in another area.

Identify specific ethical issues that create moral distress (when a person knows what is ethically appropriate but is unable to act appropriately because of various obstacles). Provide opportunities to discuss how these issues can be addressed more candidly and productively. Include nurses in discussions when physicians talk to patients about serious medical mistakes. In a study published in the January 2009 issue of *The Joint Commission Journal on Quality and Patient Safety*, the authors reported that leaving nurses out of the disclosure process may contribute to moral distress, less job satisfaction and increased turnover.

Make site visits to organizations that have won national recognition for their high patient- and staff-satisfaction rates, low nursing-vacancy rates and exceptional clinical outcomes to learn how their organizational culture has succeeded in designing and maintaining best practices.

Encourage retreats and educational opportunities that can refresh and inspire staff members to focus on compassionate care of others *and* one's self.

No healthcare executive or other healthcare professional intentionally avoids taking active steps to reduce the incidence of compassion fatigue. However, we must not ignore the high costs associated with compassion fatigue, both in terms of quality of care and financial impact. These costs may not be easy to measure precisely, but we need not wait for more definitive analyses to appreciate their ramifications.

Ideally, compassion should be demonstrated regularly and consistently. When Thomas M. Tierney was director of the Social Security Administration's bureau of health insurance more than 25 years ago he said, "law cannot create values or commitment, conscience cannot be legislated and compassion cannot be purchased." His sentiments are still valid today. Our challenge is to make certain these priceless virtues are present in all our institutions.

Originally published in the September/October 2009 issue of *Healthcare Executive* magazine.

Discussion Questions

Numerous reasons are cited for compassion fatigue. Identify four you believe are most significant and provide your reasoning.

Explain which steps proposed by the author would be most likely to reduce compassion fatigue.

Ethical Uncertainty and Staff Stress Services

William A. Nelson, PhD, HFACHE

ETHICAL UNCERTAINTY AND CONFLICTS are encountered regularly by both healthcare executives and clinicians. There is a growing understanding that organizational and clinical ethical conflicts have a significant detrimental impact on today's healthcare organizations in many ways, affecting an organization's culture, quality of care, and potential for success.

Examples of the potentially harmful impact ethical conflicts can make on an organization include:

- **Staff:** caregiver stress, deflated morale, job turnover
- **Patients:** poor patient satisfaction, fewer self-referrals
- **Organizational culture:** diminished quality of care and professionalism
- **Relationship with community:** weakened organizational image, public relations and philanthropic giving
- **Legal:** increased litigation and settlements
- **Regulations:** negatively influencing adherence to Joint Commission and other regulatory organization standards
- **Organization's bottom line:** operational costs, diverted staff time, staff turnover; legal costs, settlements and malpractice premiums; and public relations and marketing costs, repairing public image and loss of self-referrals in

competitive markets (Nelson, W. A., W. B. Weeks, and J. M. Campfield. 2008. "The Organizational Costs of Ethical Conflicts." *Journal of Healthcare Management* 53 (1): 41–52).

MORAL DISTRESS

Staff members' moral distress is a major dimension of ethical conflicts. It appears that nurses in particular are affected by the phenomenon when dealing with the uncertainty surrounding ethical challenges. Andrew Jameton, PhD, a professor in the College of Public Health at the University of Nebraska Medical Center, first described moral distress among nurses in a nursing ethics book more than 20 years ago, but the issue has since received limited attention and is rarely discussed. Moral distress has primarily been associated with clinicians, but healthcare executives, managers, and staff members also can experience such distress.

There are several factors contributing to moral distress. One factor is ethical uncertainty, a situation in which a staff member is uncertain about the ethically appropriate course of action to take. The healthcare professional may keep this uncertainty to himself and not share his stress because he thinks he is alone in his uncertainty.

There also are situations in which the healthcare professional does raise ethics questions but feels unsupported in acknowledging her uncertainty and is without an available resource to share and discuss the issue. In both examples, the staff members feel alone in their uncertainty. In such situations, healthcare professionals can feel discouraged, frustrated, and isolated as they wrestle internally with their moral distress.

A different form of moral distress occurs when a healthcare professional knows or believes he knows the ethically appropriate course of action to take but is unable to carry out the action because of an organizational obstacle. The obstacle could be a supervisor, physician, or executive authority; lack of staff time; or legal or organizational constraints.

An obvious example is the nurse providing aggressive care, as ordered by the physician or the patient's family, while believing such a level of care is inappropriate in the given situation. Despite his misgivings, the nurse continues to treat the patient, leading to frustration, anger, and moral distress. Over a period of time moral distress can influence the staff member's morale, confidence, sense of purpose, integrity, and respect for the organization.

The findings from an empirical study using a moral distress scale noted a significant relationship between moral distress and staff satisfaction. In addition, 17 percent of the nurse respondents had left a nursing position and 28 percent considered leaving because of moral distress. The authors also noted the following relationship: the higher the level of moral distress the greater the likelihood of leaving a position (Hamric, A. B., and L. J. Blackwell. 2007. "Nurse–Physician Perspectives on the Care of Dying Patients in Intensive Care Units: Collaboration, Moral Distress, and Ethical Climate." *Critical Care Medicine* 35 (2): 422–29).

These findings confirm the perceptions and experiences of many in the healthcare field—that moral distress is real and can have a negative impact on healthcare professionals, the quality of care, and, due to high job turnover rates, the organization's overall financial situation.

DECREASING MORAL DISTRESS

Many factors can contribute to moral distress in the vertical hierarchy in which most clinicians and administrators function. These factors include differences in personal and professional values, organizational pressures, the lack of an effective ethics program promoting ethical practices, and lack of an ethical culture throughout an organization. To manage and potentially decrease the presence of moral distress and its negative effect on staff, organizations should take the following steps.

First, recognize that staff stress, morale issues, and even job turnover occurring in the organization may actually be the result of moral distress and ethical conflicts. Staff members should be self-aware of the phenomena and seek assistance. Equally, staff members should recognize signs of moral distress in colleagues. Recognizing moral distress can lead to constructive approaches for managing it.

Second, ensure an environment exists in which ethical questions or uncertainty can be openly shared and discussed. Leaders must create a culture in which all staff feel comfortable and safe to raise their ethical concerns, free from any retribution.

Third, ensure the organization's ethics committee is readily available to all staff members and that all are aware of how to access the committee. Ethics committee members should be knowledgeable about and skilled at addressing a broad range of potential ethical challenges, including organizational, management, research and quality improvement issues, besides the traditional clinical issues.

In addition to a reactive approach to moral distress, ethics committees should implement a proactive approach. Committee members should reach out to the various units of the organization and lead discussions to explore the scope and causes of recurring ethical challenges that create moral distress for the staff. Such discussions could lead to development of ethics practice strategies to address and possibly decrease the stressful nature of ethical conflicts.

Lastly, organizations need to ensure employee health programs are readily available to staff. Employees should be able to use these programs to discuss—in a confidential setting—emotional issues arising in the work environment.

Moral distress is real and has a negative effect on healthcare organizations. Healthcare leaders need to acknowledge this reality and, in conjunction with their ethics program leadership, develop and implement specific strategies for addressing the issue.

Originally published in the July/August 2009 issue of *Healthcare Executive* magazine.

Discussion Questions

Explain how the presence of clinical ethics conflicts can create moral destress.

The author highlights the significant impact of moral distress on healthcare professionals. What do you believe is the impact on the organization?

Selected Bibliography

Adelman, J. 2019. "High Reliability Healthcare: Building Safer Systems Through Just Culture and Technology." *Journal of Healthcare Management* 64 (3): 137–41.

American Society for Bioethics and Humanities (ASBH). 1998. *Core Competencies for Healthcare Ethics Consultation*. Glenview, IL: ASBH.

Asch, D., and P. Ubel. 1997. "Rationing by Any Other Name." *New England Journal of Medicine* 336 (23): 1668–71.

Aulisio, M., R. Arnold, and S. Youngner. 2000. "Health Care Ethics Consultation: Nature, Goals, and Competencies." *Annals of Internal Medicine* 133 (1): 59–69.

Beauchamp, T. L., and J. F. Childress. 2019. *Principles of Biomedical Ethics*. New York: Oxford University Press.

Berlinger, N., B. Jennings, and S. Wolf. 2013. *The Hastings Center Guidelines for Decisions on Life-Sustaining Treatment and Care Near the End of Life*. Oxford, UK: Oxford University Press.

Blacksher, E., and S. Valles. 2021. "White Privilege, White Poverty: Reckoning with Class and Race in America." *Hastings Center Report* 51 (1): S51–S57.

Blake, D. C. 2000. "Reinventing the Healthcare Ethics Committee." *HEC Forum* 12 (1): 8–32.

Boyle, P., and E. Moskowitz. 1996. "Making Tough Resource Decisions." *Health Progress* 77 (6): 48–53.

Byock, I. 2010. "Dying with Dignity." *Hastings Center Report* 40 (2): inside back cover.

Brock, D. W. 2008. "Conscientious Refusal by Physicians and Pharmacists: Who Is Obligated to Do What, and Why?" *Theories of Medical Bioethics* 29 (3): 187–200.

Brody, H. 2012. "From an Ethics of Rationing to an Ethics of Waste Avoidance." *New England Journal of Medicine* 366 (21): 1949–51.

Brudney, D. 2019. "Changing the Question." *Hastings Center Report* 49 (2): 9–16.

Callahan, D. 2000. "Rationing, Equity, and Affordable Care." *Health Progress* 81 (4): 38–41.

Campbell, K., and K. Parsi. 2017. "The New Age of Patient Transparency." *Healthcare Executive* 32 (6): 40, 42–43.

Celie, K. B., and K. Prager. 2016. "Health Care Ethics Consultation in the United States." *AMA Journal of Ethics* 18 (5): 475–78.

Cochran, C., J. Kupersmith, and T. McGovern. 2000. "Justice, Allocation, and Managed Care." *Health Progress* 81 (4): 34–37, 41.

Cohen, J. G. 2010. "Medical Tourism: The View from Ten Thousand Feet." *Hastings Center Report* 40 (2): 11–12.

Cook, A. F., and K. Guttmannova. 2002. "Ethical Issues Faced by Rural Physicians." *South Dakota Journal of Medicine* 55 (6): 221–24.

Cook, A. F., and H. Hoas. 2000. "Bioethics Activities in Rural Hospitals." *Cambridge Quarterly of Healthcare Ethics* 9 (2): 230–38.

———. 2000. "Where the Rubber Hits the Road: Implications for Organizational and Clinical Ethics in Rural Healthcare Settings." *HEC Forum* 12 (4): 331–40.

Crigger, B.-J. 1995. "Negotiating the Moral Order: Paradoxes of Ethics Consultation." *Kennedy Institute of Ethics Journal* 5 (2): 89–112.

Crisp, N. 2020. *Health Is Made at Home: Hospitals Are for Repairs.* Essex, UK: SALUS Global Knowledge Exchange.

Daniels, N. 1986. "Why Saying No to Patients in the United States Is So Hard." *New England Journal of Medicine* 314 (21): 1380–83.

DeMartino, E., and J. Rolnick. 2019. "The States as Laboratories: Regulation of Decisions for Incapacitated Patients." *Journal of Clinical Ethics* 30 (2): 89–95.

DeRenzo, E. 2019. "Moving Towards a New Hospital Model of Clinical Ethics." *Journal of Clinical Ethics* 30 (2): 121–27.

DeRenzo, E., P. Panzarella, S. Selinger, and J. Schwartz. 2005. "Emancipation, Capacity, and the Difference Between Law and Ethics." *Journal of Clinical Ethics* 16 (2): 144–50.

Diekema, D. M., M. Mercurio, and M. Adam (eds.). 2011. *Clinical Ethics in Pediatrics: A Case-Based Textbook.* Cambridge, UK: Cambridge University Press.

Doherty, R., and R. Purtilo. 2016. *Ethical Dimensions in the Health Professions.* Philadelphia, PA: Elsevier Press.

Dubler, N., and C. Liebman. 2011. *Bioethics Mediation: A Guide to Shaping Shared Solutions.* Nashville, TN: Vanderbilt University Press.

Edwards, A., G. Elwyn, and R. Thompson (eds.). 2016. *Shared Decision Making in Health Care*. New York: Oxford University Press.

Edwards, K., and R. Newman. 2020. "Physician Burnout and Ethics Committees." *Journal of Clinical Ethics* 31 (1): 42–47.

Egener, B. E., D. J. Mason, W. J. McDonald, S. Okun, M. E. Gaines, D. A. Fleming, B. M. Rosof, D. Gullen, and M. L. Andresen. 2017. "The Charter on Professionalism for Health Care Organizations." *Academic Medicine* 92 (8): 1091–99.

Elwyn, G., D. Frosch, R. Thomson, N. Joseph-Williams, A. Lloyd, P. Kinnersley, E. Cording, D. Thomson, C. Dodd, S. Rollnick, E. Edwards, and M. Berry. 2012. "Shared Decision Making: A Model for Clinical Practice." *Journal of General Internal Medicine* 27 (10): 1361–67.

Epner, P. L., and D. Siegal. 2019. "An Urgent Call for Leaders to Support More Accurate and Timely Diagnosis." *Journal of Healthcare Management* 64 (6): 359–62.

Fineberg, H. V. 2017. "Conflict of Interest: Why Does It Matter?" *JAMA* 317 (17): 1717–18.

Fletcher, J., P. Lombardo, and E. Spencer. 2005. *Fletcher's Introduction to Clinical Ethics*, 3rd ed. Hagerstown, MD: University Publishing Group.

Ford, P., and D. Dudzinski (eds.). 2008. *Complex Ethics Consultations: Cases That Haunt Us*. Cambridge, UK: Cambridge University Press.

Friesen, P. 2020. "Medically Assisted Dying and Suicide: How Are They Different, and How Are They Similar?" *Hastings Center Report* 50 (1): 32–43.

Glover, J. J. 2001. "Rural Bioethical Issues of the Elderly: How Do They Differ from Urban Ones?" *Journal of Rural Health* 17 (4): 332–35.

Gold, A. 2010. "Physicians' 'Right of Conscience'—Beyond Politics." *Journal of Law, Medicine, and Ethics* 38 (1): 134–42.

Guildry-Grimes, L., M. Warren, H. Lipman, K. Kent, K. B. Krishnamurthy, A. Davis, T. May, M. Jiro, and J. Jankowski. 2019. "Clarifying a Clinical Ethics Service's Value, the Visible and the Hidden." *Journal of Clinical Ethics* 30 (3): 251–61.

Hester, D. M., and T. Schonfeld. 2012. *Guidance for Healthcare Ethics Committees.* Cambridge, UK: Cambridge University Press.

Hilfiker, D. 1984. "Facing Our Mistakes." *New England Journal of Medicine* 310 (2): 118–22.

Hoffman, S. 2019. "Physician Burnout Calls for Legal Intervention." *Hastings Center Report* 49 (6): 8–9.

Hofmann, P. 2020. "Rapidly Accelerating Use of Artificial Intelligence and Robotics Demands Ethical Analysis." *Patient Safety and Quality Healthcare* 17 (2): 20–22.

Hofmann, P. 2006. "When Patients Make 'Unwise' Decisions." *Hospitals & Health Networks Online*, June 13.

Hofmann, P., and L. Schneiderman. 2007. "Physicians Should Not Always Pursue a Good 'Clinical' Outcome." *Hastings Center Report* 37 (3): inside back cover.

Howe, E. 2020. "Beyond Determining Decision-Making Capacity." *Journal of Clinical Ethics* 31 (1): 3–16.

———. 2000. "Leaving Luputa: What Doctors Aren't Taught About Informed Consent." *Journal of Clinical Ethics* 11 (1): 3–13.

Institute of Medicine. 1999. *To Err Is Human: Building a Safer Health System.* Washington, DC: Institute of Medicine and National Academy Press.

Jennings, B. 2016. "Reconceptualizing Autonomy: A Relational Turn in Bioethics." *Hastings Center Report* 46 (3): 11–16.

Jonsen, A., M. Siegler, and W. Winslade. 2015. *Clinical Ethics: A Practical Approach to Ethical Decisions in Clinical Medicine,* 8th ed. New York: McGraw-Hill.

Kan Yin Li, J. 2020. "Rethinking the Assessment of Decision-Making Capacity and Making Treatment-Related Decisions." *Journal of Clinical Ethics* 31 (1): 60–67.

Kelly, S. E., P. A. Marshall, L. M. Sanders, T. A. Raffin, and B. A. Koenig. 1997. "Understanding the Practice of Ethics Consultation: Results of an Ethnographic Multi-Site Study." *Journal of Clinical Ethics* 8 (2): 136–49.

Lo, B. 2019. *Resolving Ethical Dilemmas: A Guide for Clinicians.* Philadelphia, PA: Lippincott Williams & Wilkins.

Lown, B., A. Shin, and R. Jones. 2019. "Can Organizational Leaders Sustain Compassionate, Patient-Centered Care and Mitigate Burnout?" *Journal of Healthcare Management* 64 (6): 398–412.

Martone, M. 2002. "Decision-Making Issues in the Rehabilitation Process." *Hastings Center Report* 31 (2): 36–41.

Mazur, D. J., D. H. Hikam, M. D. Mazur, and M. D. Mazur. 2005. "The Role of Doctor's Opinion in Shared Decision Making: What Does Shared Decision Making Really Mean When Considering Invasive Medical Procedures?" *Health Expectations* 8 (2): 97–102.

Menser, T., and B. Gregory. 2018. "An Organizational Intervention to Reduce Physician Burnout." *Journal of Healthcare Management* 63 (5): 338–52.

Miller, F., and A. Wertheimer. 2007. "Facing Up to Paternalism in Research Ethics." *Hastings Center Report* 37 (3): 24–34.

Moulton, B., and J. King. 2010. "Aligning Ethics with Medical Decision-Making: The Quest for Informed Patient Choice." *Journal of Law, Medicine, and Ethics* 38 (1): 85–97.

Nelson, W. A. (ed.). 2010. *Handbook for Rural Health Care Ethics: A Practical Guide for Professionals.* Lebanon, NH: Dartmouth College Press.

Nelson, W. A., and W. B. Weeks. 2008. "The Organizational Costs of Ethical Conflicts." *Journal of Healthcare Management* 53 (1): 41–52.

Nelson, W. A., P. J. Barr, and M. Castaldo. 2015. "The Opportunities and Challenges for Shared Decision-Making in the Rural United States." *HEC Forum* 27 (2): 157–70.

Nelson, W. A., P. Gardent, E. Shulman, and M. Splaine. 2010. "Preventing Ethics Conflicts and Improving Healthcare Quality Through System Redesign." *Quality and Safety in Health Care* 19 (3): 526–30.

Nelson, W. A., W. B. Weeks, and J. M. Campfield. 2008. "The Organizational Costs of Ethical Conflicts." *Journal of Healthcare Management* 53 (1): 41–52.

National Academies of Sciences, Engineering, and Medicine. 2019. *Taking Action Against Clinician Burnout: A Systems Approach to Professional Well-Being.* Washington, DC: National Academies Press.

Ogrinc, G., W. A. Nelson, S. M. Adams, and A. E. O'Hara. 2013. "An Instrument to Differentiate Between Clinical Research and Quality Improvement." *IRB: Ethics & Human Research* 35 (5): 1–8.

Pearlman, R. A., M. B. Foglia, E. Fox, J. H. Cohen, B. L. Chanko, and K. A. Berkowitz. 2016. "Ethics Consultation Quality Assessment Tool: A Novel Method for Assessing the Quality of Ethics Case Consultations Based on Written Records." *American Journal of Bioethics* 16 (3): 3–14.

Powers, M., and R. Faden. 2000. "Inequalities in Healthcare: Four Generations of Discussion About Justice and Cost-Effectiveness Analysis." *Kennedy Institute of Ethics Journal* 10 (2): 109–27.

Rhodes, R. 1998. "Futility and the Goals of Medicine." *Journal of Clinical Ethics* 9 (2): 194–205.

Roberts, L. W., J. Battaglia, and R. S. Epstein. 1999. "Frontier Ethics: Mental Health Care Needs and Ethical Dilemmas in Rural Communities." *Psychiatric Services* 50 (4): 497–503.

Roberts, L. W., J. Battaglia, M. Smithpeter, and R. S. Epstein. 1999. "An Office on Main Street: Health Care Dilemmas in Small Communities." *Hastings Center Report* 29 (4): 28–37.

Rubin, S. B., and L. Zoloth (eds.). 2000. *Margin of Error: The Ethics of Mistakes in the Practice of Medicine.* Hagerstown, MD: University Publishing.

Shanafelt, T., S. Swensen, J. Woody, J. Levin, and J. Lillie. 2018. "Physician and Nurse Well-Being: Seven Things Hospital Boards Should Know." *Journal of Healthcare Management* 63 (6): 363–69.

Sharpe, V. A. 2003. "Promoting Patient Safety: An Ethical Basis for Policy Deliberation." *Hastings Center Report Special Supplement* 33 (5): S1–S20.

Shashidhara, S., and S. Kirk. 2020. "Moral Distress: A Framework for Offering Relief Through Debrief." *Journal of Clinical Ethics* 31 (4): 364–71.

Siegler, M. 2019. "Clinical Medical Ethics: Its History and Contributions to American Medicine." *Journal of Clinical Ethics* 30 (1): 17–26.

Smith, M., and H. Forster. 2000. "Morally Managing Medical Mistakes." *Cambridge Quarterly of Healthcare Ethics* 9 (1): 38–53.

Solovy, A. 1999. "The Price of Dignity." *Hospitals & Health Networks* 73 (3): 30.

Sparrow, R., and J. Hatherley. 2020. "High Hopes for 'Deep Medicine'? AI, Economics, and the Future of Care." *Hastings Center Report* 50 (1): 14–17.

Sulmasy, L. S., and T. Bledsoe. 2019. "American College of Physicians Ethics Manual: Seventh Edition." *Annals of Internal Medicine* 170: S1–S32.

Tarzian, A. J., and ASBH Core Competencies Update Task Force. 2013. "Health Care Ethics Consultation: An Update on Core Competencies and Emerging Standards from the American Society for Bioethics and Humanities." *American Journal of Bioethics* 13 (2): 3–13.

Tarzian, A. J., L. D. Wocial, and ASBH Clinical Ethics Consultation Affairs Committee. 2015. "A Code of Ethics for Health Care Ethics Consultants: Journey to the Present and Implications for the Field." *American Journal of Bioethics* 15 (5): 38–51.

Van Dyke, M. 2019. "Battling Clinician Burnout: Fighting the Epidemic from Within." *Healthcare Executive* 34 (1): 10–12, 14–16, 18–19.

Weeks, W. B., and W. A. Nelson. 2011. "Ethical Issues Arising from Variation in Health Services Utilization at the End of Life." *Frontiers of Health Services Management* 27 (3): 17–26.

Westling, C., T. Walsh, and W. A. Nelson. 2017. "Perceived Ethics Dilemmas Among Pioneer Accountable Care Organizations." *Journal of Healthcare Management* 62 (1): 18–27.

About the Editors

 **William A. Nelson, PhD, MDiv, HFACHE,** is director of the Ethics and Human Values Program and a professor in the Dartmouth Institute for Health Policy and Clinical Practice, the Department of Medical Education and the Department of Community and Family Medicine at Dartmouth's Geisel School of Medicine. He serves as the director of multiple courses for Dartmouth's three master of public health programs and medical school, focusing on healthcare ethics. He also is an adjunct professor at New York University's Robert F. Wagner Graduate School of Public Service.

From 1986 to 1989, Dr. Nelson was a W.K. Kellogg National Leadership Fellow, studying US and international healthcare policy. In 2008–2009, he was a National Rural Health Association Leadership Fellow. He is the author of more than 125 articles and many book chapters, and the editor of several books including the *Handbook for Rural Health Care Ethics*. He was the principal investigator of several federally and state-funded research studies fostering an evidence-based approach to ethics.

Dr. Nelson has received many awards, including the US Congressional Excalibur Award for Public Service and an honorary doctorate of humane letters from his alma mater, Elmhurst College. In 2013, he was named an Honorary Fellow of the American College of Healthcare Executives (ACHE) for "his pioneering work in healthcare organization ethics." He has received the Dartmouth Institute for Health Policy and Clinical Practice's student teaching award and, in 2018, was elected to the Geisel School of Medicine's Academy of Master Educators. In 2004, the US Department of Veterans Affairs established the annual competitive William A. Nelson Award for Excellence in Health Care Ethics. He has served as the ethics adviser to ACHE's Ethics Committee since 2006.

 **Paul B. Hofmann, DrPH, LFACHE,** is president of the Hofmann Healthcare Group in Moraga, California. Although he devotes a majority of his time to pro bono activities, he continues to write, speak and consult on ethical issues in healthcare and to serve as an adviser to healthcare companies and as an expert witness.

Dr. Hofmann has served as executive director of Emory University Hospital and director of Stanford University Hospital and Clinics. For 19 years, he coordinated the annual two-day ethics seminar for the American College of Healthcare Executives (ACHE). He is coeditor of *Management Mistakes in Healthcare: Identification, Correction and Prevention*, published in 2005 by Cambridge University Press. He serves on the American Hospital Association's Quest for Quality Prize committee, the Joint Commission's international Standards Advisory Panel and the board of trustees of the Education Development Center. He is a cofounder of Operation Access and the Alliance for Global Clinical Training.

In 1976, Dr. Hofmann was the recipient of ACHE's Robert S. Hudgens Memorial Award for Young Hospital Administrator of the Year. In 2004, he received the Distinguished Leadership Award from the University of California Graduate Program in Health Management Alumni Association. He received the 2009 American Hospital Association's Award of Honor for his central role in shaping the understanding of healthcare ethics. In 2012, he was one of eight recipients of the national Schweitzer Leadership Award.

An author of more than 200 publications, Dr. Hofmann has held faculty appointments at Harvard, UCLA, Stanford, Emory, Seton Hall, and the University of California. His bachelor of science, master of public health, and doctor of public health degrees are from the University of California.

About the Contributors

Kate Clay, RN, was director of shared decision-making education and outreach at the Office of Professional Education at the Dartmouth Institute for Health Policy and Clinical Practice.

Richard A. Culbertson, PhD, MHA, MDiv, is professor and director of health policy and systems management at the Louisiana State University (LSU) School of Public Health in New Orleans, professor of family medicine at LSU and a faculty associate of the American College of Healthcare Executives.

Robert C. Macauley, MD, FAAP, is a professor of pediatrics at Oregon Health Sciences University, specializing in palliative care and ethics.

Douglas Van Houten, RN, is a retired assistant chief nursing officer, stroke program coordinator and intensive care unit nurse.